A Century of Cycling

Marking the 100th anniversary of the Leicestershire and Rutland District Association of the Cyclists' Touring Club

* * *

Compiled by Eileen Johnson and Janet Jones.

Edited by Ken Hoxley

This book is dedicated to all those
Leicestershire CTC members who
have enjoyed some time awheel
during the last 100 years

A Century of Cycling
Written and Compiled
by Eileen Johnson
and Janet Jones

* * *

Edited and published
by Ken Hoxley
9 Meadowbrook Road
Kibworth Beauchamp,
Leicester

* * *

Printed by Teamprint
Loughborough
March 1997

* * *

ISBN:

1- 871431- 08 - 5

Contents

THe CTC's new President is journalist and broadcaster Phil Liggett. Our 100th year will co-incide with his 25th consecutive year of covering the Tour de France.
He writes for the Daily and Sunday Telegraph and has covered the last seven Olympic Games for national TV around the world, including ITV and BBC. He is well known as host of the Channel 4 Tour de France daily coverage.
He is very proud of his appointment with the CTC and recalls starting his cycling career in 1960 with rides in the Wirral.

The signs are good

ONE HUNDRED years is a long time to be around in an ever changing world, but if you understand and enjoy the company of cyclists, you will understand, too, that it is no time at all. The Leicestershire and Rutland DA of the CTC epitomises why the Club has gone from strength to strength, bringing not only enjoyment to the national membership of 43,000, but through its diverse activities, safer cycling and vast enjoyment to non-members as well.

My first cycle ride was from Bebington Station on the Wirral Peninsula almost 40 years' ago (I was very young at the time!). Four hours later I had found the friendship of wonderful people and discovered the roads into Wales. Since that moment I have ridden thousands of miles and enjoyed many, many friendships around the world. Cycling became my life and has found no bounds.

When the Leicestershire and Rutland DA celebrates throughout 1997, it will be a time to reflect, but not to grow complacent, as the pastime faces many problems on our crowded roads. There are signs at last that councils and government are recognising that roads cannot continue to be built using vast tracts of countryside to satisfy the endless tentacles of the motorist. Soon we, as cyclists will enjoy the benefits that will eventually come from this realisation.

I will be with you on some of the rides and look forward to the selfish pleasure I will get from meandering around the many lanes of Leicestershire and Rutland, talking old times with new friends.
Enjoy the 100th year - we won't be around for the next!

PHIL LIGGETT
CTC President

Memories are made of this

by Ken Hoxley

THIS book does not really claim to be an official history of the Leicestershire and Rutland District Association, but, as the title suggests, it is the both the story and a celebration of a century of cycle riding by its members. Of course many details of historic interest are recorded, but in the main we have sought to obtain a kaleidoscope of memories. Some of the contributors - and readers - have enjoyed many years membership while others may, as yet, have had only a mild flirtation with this great pastime.

The very fact that you are reading this suggests you have an interest in riding on two wheels (or perhaps three) with the added satisfaction that comes from having accomplished getting from A to B and back again entirely under your own steam. No matter what branch of the pastime your enjoy, be it racing, touring, or just pottering around the lanes on your own, we hope you will find something of interest in the many anecdotes..

I moved to Leicestershire 25 years ago and I consider myself a comparative newcomer. Some of the characters and locations are unknown to me, but I've been a cyclist for almost 50 years and can recognise (and recall) many similar situations. They are the sort of scrapes and experiences which are repeated wherever cyclists gather to ride in company. Some the stories will make you chuckle, and no doubt the many names of clubfolk mentioned will conjure up varying memories of them. Enjoy sharing these moments, and if you have been in "retirement" from the game, it might just inspire you to rescue that old machine from the shed, dust it down and take it for a spin up the road.

The CTC is, of course, primarily a touring organisation. I say primarily because in recent months there have been suggestions that the club should embrace, and indeed control, certain aspects of cycling racing.

If that happens, in 100 years' time members will look back on even more varied and enjoyable memories. In his introduction, CTC president Phil Liggett says that we won't be around to celebrate the double centenary. That's true, but hopefully some of our very younger members will be around for a large proportion of it.

No praise can be too high for Eileen Johnson. This book was her dream and it became a personal challenge. She had in her mind a picture of the finished product she wanted and kept the rest of us hard at it, setting almost impossible deadlines. One can only marvel at her great enthusiasm. She had able assistance from Janet Jones, a newcomer to cycling, who was anxious to hone her literary skills by assisting with interviewing and writing. She was able to keep a non-biased eye on everything.

We've burned a lot of midnight oil in producing this book, hopefully you'll think it has all been worthwhile.

How it all began

The Cyclists Touring Club was founded on 5th August 1878 and although Leicestershire members were active in the formative years of the club - it was not until 18 years later that a Leicester section was actually formed. It followed an appeal in the CTC Gazette from J Edwin Roper, of Southfields, Leicester, who was Chief Consul for the County. This automatically made him a member of the CTC National Council and there is little doubt that he played a great part in the formation of the Leicestershire District Association.

Mr Roper explained that his aim in forming a district section was "to allow the 317 members of the area the opportunity of becoming personally acquainted. Membership had increased from 186 earlier in the year and now included 52 ladies."

As a result of the appeal, local CTC members met on Saturday 19th September 1896 at the Tram Terminus, London Road, Knighton, for a ride to Glen Magna, Wistow and Kilby. Fifty members, including 16 ladies, were met at Wistow Park by Col. Sir H. Halford Bart. who was himself a new member of the CTC. A commemorative photograph was taken with Sir Henry in the centre. Unfortunately he was seated on his horse rather than on his bicycle, but nevertheless he was warmly greeted.

The second run took place on Saturday 3rd October 1896 when 60 members, several of whom were ladies, met at Belgrave Church to ride up Mowmacre Hill to Thurcaston, around the reservoir to Swithland, one of the prettiest rides in the county, with tea "partaken of at Woodhouse Eaves." The run then continued to Loughborough before returning to Leicester via Quorn and Belgrave. "Rain at the start lessened the attendance, but it soon cleared leaving the roads in splendid condition."

A meeting of Leicestershire members was held at the Wyvern Temperance Hotel on Wednesday 17th March 1897. The Chief Consul presided and was supported by Messrs A Goodwin, J Dulley, and TJ Powell, consuls for Kegworth, Market Harborough and Wigston respectively. Among those present were Messrs B Baldwin GW Armstrong, C Stretton, JC Burton, GL Berry, FL Wale, GE Simons, JW Patey, A Bassett, F Barlow, R Barber, CW Findley and C Potter.

The chief consul gave an account of work undertaken since the formation of the Leicester District Section last autumn and referred to his negotiations for the abolition of dangerous gates across public roads. It was resolved to approach the Midland Railway as to the issue of special tickets for members for day tours, partly by train and partly by road. A list of runs was drawn up and it was agreed to meet monthly on Saturdays and Thursdays (meeting in each case at Granville Road, Leicester). A minimum subscription of 1/- from those joining these Leicester District Section outings was to be used to defray incidental expenses. A vote of thanks to the consuls for their efforts on behalf of the members concluded the proceedings.

From all this, some idea of the enthusiasm of local members can be gained as they entered the year in which they were to become a district association. The CTC Gazette of June 1897 included a letter from J Edwin Roper giving notice of his intention to apply to the CTC Council for permission to form a district association in the county of Leicester.

As a result, at the monthly council meeting, held at the George Hotel, Shrewsbury on Saturday 14th August 1897, the CTC Council resolved - "Item 165 - That the council do hereby sanction the formation of a district association for the county of Leicester." Incidentally, items 166 and 167 were also resolved for Nottingham and Lothian respectively.

Subsequently, at a meeting held at the George Hotel, Haymarket, Leicester on Tuesday 14th September 1897, chaired by J Edwin Roper "Acting upon the sanction of the council granted at the Shrewsbury meeting" a resolution was unanimously passed forming a district association for the county of Leicester." The meeting then elected a committee and adopted a constitution, embodying the objects set forth in the report of the district association committee to the council at Newcastle-upon-Tyne and published in the May 1897 issue of the Gazette. Several other resolutions were also passed by way of instruction to the local committee in drawing up the constitution and rules of the association and starting it upon a sound basis.

The committee comprised: the Chief Consul, J Edwin Roper and representative councillor, HW Orton, ex-officio. GL Berry (secretary and treasurer): TJ Webb (Loughborough consul) A Goodwin (Kegworth consul): T Dent (Melton consul) : J Dulley Jnr (Market Harborough consul): for the county J Staynes, F Barlow and WG Chapman: for the city R Barber.

The official inaugural ride of the association was at 2.45pm on Saturday 18th September 1897 from Granville Road near to Victoria Park pavilion. They rode to Wistow Park via Glen Magna (now known as Great Glen) with tea at the Bath Hotel, Shearsby. The return was via Wigston and Oadby. The first meeting of the committee was at the house of the Chief Consul in West Street, Southfields, when it was reported that the run to Wistow Park and Shearsby was much enjoyed, several ladies participating.

Runs for October 1897 were as follows:

Saturday 9th Oct.	Market Harborough	Tea Peacock Hotel
Thursday 14th Oct	Billesdon	Tea White Hart Hotel
Saturday 16th Oct	Lutterworth	Tea Hind Hotel
Thursday 21st Oct	Melton Mowbray	Tea George Hotel

Saturday 23rd Oct	Hinckley	Tea Union Hotel
Thursday 28th Oct	Wistow Park	Tea Bath Hotel
Saturday 30th Oct	Bradgate Park	Tea Bradgate Hotel

At the November meeting, J Edwin Roper resigned as Chief Consul, blaming other pressing commitments. He was succeeded by BS Baldwin, of Leicester. At a later meeting Mr Roper was presented with an illuminated address in appreciation of his work.

The first secretary/treasurer, George Berry of Aylestone, held office for ten years, but stood down as secretary in 1907. He continued as treasurer for a short while. A dinner to celebrate the DA's 10th anniversary, was held at Winn's Oriental Cafe, Market Place, Leicester. A handsomely bound book on gardening, together with a list of subscribers and a purse containing the balance of subscriptions, was presented to George by the chairman, Mr F Barlow.

Following the presentation and subsequent speeches, the remainder of the evening was "spent in harmony" and the following gentlemen favoured the company with songs and recitations, Messrs Earp (Sen and Jnr), FA Barlow, WH Orton, AG Bakewell, and BL M'Quillin.

Historical note: George Berry was born in Devon about 1859. We have no idea when he came to Leicestershire, but he was one of the members at the Wyvern Temperance Hotel meeting on 17th March 1897. Shortly after resigning as secretary, he also relinquished the treasurer's job and moved to Norfolk to start a small market garden. The next reference we find is on 8th February 1909 when the committee sent a letter of sympathy on hearing he was dangerously ill. He died shortly after this. The bound gardening book was loaned to the DA during the production of both this book, and a previous record, prepared by John Allen for the 90th anniversary. It is indeed a worthy heirloom for his descendants.

At the AGM on 12th March 1908 Rutland was incorporated with the Leicestershire DA. Before this Rutland came under the auspices of Nottingham DA. The title Leicestershire and Rutland DA was maintained until the reorganisation of the county structures by central government in the 1970s, after which the title reverted to Leicestershire DA. Now, in 1997, central government has again 'reorganised' and the committee are busy changing bank accounts, etc., back to the name Leicestershire and Rutland DA.

AW Wilkinson succeeded George Berry as secretary in 1907 and continued to serve on the committee for many years. The Gazette of January 1915 had a piece by the then secretary, BL M'Quillin which read "Mr AW Wilkinson, well known locally as the founder of the Leicester Road Club - a club 'par excellence' of the speed brigade - has joined a cyclists' battalion. He is a member of our committee and we wish him a safe return. Mr Norman, another 'speedman' is already at the front as a motor cycle despatch rider."

At the outbreak of the First World War in 1914 an appeal had been made for cyclists to offer their services in some active form. "All who can join the Army, the Territorial Force, the Cycling Battalions etc. should do so at once........Of those unable to join, it is proposed to register names under two classes (a) for home defence (full time) and (b) for non-militant National Service (part time).

TJ Webb, consul for Loughborough, and a member of the first committee formed on 14th September 1897, became the first President in 1900 until handing over to CH Garner in 1918. Bernard M'Quillin became secretary in 1913 and continued as such for the next 11 years. When he stood down, in 1924, the DA bought him a lightweight bike which cost £3 (referred to in the chapter on Bill Seager).

Bernard M'Quillin became President in 1925 and served until 1931 a long record of service to the DA. He was active in the DA from the early 1900s at least, being recorded, in copperplate handwriting, as a subscriber to GL Berry's bound book in 1907.

At the AGM held on 14th March 1917 at the office of TJ Webb with members present from Barrow on Soar, Leicester, Loughborough and Nottingham, "Mr Masser wished it to be made known among the membership that clubmen on active service remained on the roll, though their subscription be unpaid" National Office had agreed to waive subscription fees in these cases. "The secretary was instructed to write to the members thus affected"

JT Masser (Nottingham) was national representative councillor for the area from 1902 until 1924 and was also Leicestershire DA's consulting solicitor. He rarely missed a meeting during this time.

At a committee meeting on Wednesday 9th January 1918, held at the Old Town Hall, Leicester, the runs' secretary was congratulated upon his marriage. This was the first wedding of a club official for 14 years and it was reported that "the new benedict was to receive a gift of books, chosen by himself, to commemorate his rash act. These were subscribed for by his friends." (Leicester had the doubtful distinction of having the greatest percentage of bachelors in Great Britain, this despite the girls outnumbering the men three to one).

Mrs Barker, of 149 Main St, Mountsorrel, complained that the village food committee had declined to register her as a caterer, thereby rendering it extremely difficult, or perhaps impossible, to provide rest and refreshment for weary travellers and mud stained cyclists. The committee decided to approach the responsible authority on her behalf, calling on them to reconsider their untenable position. Failing success, the club's head office should be asked to step in.

Bernard M'Quillin, the secretary, was a real character, keeping brake blocks in his pocket to stop them wearing out and putting on two pair of shorts to hide the holes in the first pair. He was a legend in his own lifetime and took part in the 60th DA anniversary ride on Saturday 21st September 1957 alongside another 'great' CTC national vice president, Bill Oakley. The AGM on 6th February 1918 declined to accept Chief Consul Webb's plea of longevity and expressed the hope that he would continue to hold and adorn the offices he had for many years so efficiently filled. However, the committee which sat on 4th June 1919 accepted with regret the resignation of Mr Webb. A vote of thanks was passed and it was ordered that a copy be sent to this veteran cyclist.

Mr Webb said he had been a member for 40 years and had served as Chief Consul for half that period, and had been a member of council for 11 years. He hoped to remain a member until the last (applause).

The following is a excerpt from the CTC Gazette of September 1920:

Organised by the Leicestershire and Rutland DA in conjunction with the local centres of the NCU, the second North Midland Rally proved an immense success and one desire of the promoters, to show the public that our glorious pastime is very much alive, was most certainly achieved.

The rendezvous chosen was the same as last year, viz. Normanton on Soar, and in the matter of charming situation and surroundings no spot could be more delightful than this riverside village. The various contingents began to converge on the yard of The Plough' early in the afternoon and were kept busy by the 'camera fiend' for a considerable time.

Some 135 participated in the rally, of whom about 100 sat down to an excellent tea, following which a Lighting Regulation protest meeting was held on the lawn. A Nottingham veteran, Mr. Sowter, presided and the following resolution was proposed by Mr BL M'Quillin in an extremely able, witty and telling speech:

"That this gathering of cyclists emphatically protests against the continued imposition of the purely war-time Lighting Regulations made under the Defence of the Realm Act, involving the carrying at night of a red rear light by cycles and the lighting up of both lamps one half hour after sunset; and calls upon the Government, in the name of the great majority of cyclists and pedestrians in this country, to cancel such regulations forthwith and so restore the pre-war lighting laws."

The motion was seconded by Mr Albert Eld of Leicester and carried nem. con. It was decided to send copies of this resolution to every Member of Parliament for the three Counties of Notts, Derbys and Leics and also to the Home Secretary and the Minister of Transport.

It will be interesting to see what replies, if any, are made by these gentlemen.

Before 1922 there was only a single DA run, with members from outlying districts joining at lunch or tea. Frequent joint events were successfully held with neighbouring DAs. Communications were good and a members word was his bond. If meals were booked they stayed booked! At the AGM on 4th January 1922 - Silver Jubilee Year - it was agreed that a Loughborough runs' section be formed. Mr EE Worthy of 111 Ratcliffe Road, Loughborough, became secretary. FCW Stevenson, of Barrow on Soar, Chief Consul after TJ Webb, was very active in forming this new section and led some of the runs. Later that year Leicester A B and C sections were formed. It was around this period that DAs were adopting club colours. Leicestershire's choice of red and white has now been in being for more than 70 years.

An abbreviated history from that time starts with the opening of a new clubroom at the Turkey Cafe, Granby St., Leicester on 12th October 1923. The impressive facade is still there, but is no longer a cafe. AGMs were held there for some years.

Arthur Mabbut, his wife and friends on a section run in the 1920s

1924: Saw the beginning of many of today's DA standard events. The first map reading and first 120miles in 12 hours.

1925: The standard ride became 130 miles in 12 hours (100 miles in 12 hours for the ladies). Ladies were also given their own rally on 13th June. Thirty seven ladies attended and proceeded to Normanton on Soar, escorted by some men. A further party of men joined them for tea in a riverside garden, bringing the total number of riders to 90.

1927: TJ Webb died on 28th January in Llandudno, severing an important link with the early days of the club. On 10th December the DA beat the Keir Hardie Wheelers (now Leicester Forest CC) by six clear goals thus maintaining their unbeaten record at football.

1928: Golden Jubilee Year of the CTC. 3rd March, another victory at football over the Keir Hardy Wheelers; 6th March, Jubilee Dance; Tuesday 12th and Wednesday 13th June, the CTC Round Britain Relay Ride came to Leicestershire. "A crowd of townsfolk witnessed their arrival at the Town Hall where the Mayor appended his signature. Leicestershire DA were responsible from Stamford to Leicester. Their team, four men and one lady experienced torrential rain between Uppingham and Leicester and had serious tyre trouble. They were congratulated on keeping the ultimate loss of time down to 11 minutes. The following morning, another team of five men left the Town Hall just before 6.30am and arrived at Loughborough 50 minutes later, five minutes behind time. With the addition of the signature of Loughborough Mayor, Mr Alan Moss, the roll was carried forward to Shardlow where Derby DA took over.

1929: A committee was formed to consider a DA monthly bulletin.

1930: Active sections - Hardriders, Generals, Socials, Sunday Half Day. Miss MK Kirk stands down as Chief Consul.

1931: Chief Consul Mr C Fisher. 12th/13th September - Inter DA Rally at Spring Hill Farm, Whitwick. Camping section formed.

1932: Hinckley section formed, secretary Mr C Wells. 1933 Cycle Chat first published.

1934: Eighty eight members present at the AGM held at Secular Hall on 12th January. Sections now active: Social, Loiterers, General, Camping, Thursday evening, Tandem and Hinckley.

1935: Intermediate section formed.

1936: Throughout its history, until the trams finished, the termini were used as starting points. However, a letter from Leicester Corporation Tramway Dept. asked the DA not to stick their runs labels onto the overhead wire standards. (upright cast iron pillars).

1937: Members present at first committee meeting on 2nd February Whitemore, Gannon, Mrs Kath Nickels, Flavell, Goodwin, Thomas, Markham, Turner, Allen, Hales, Record, Seager, Warner, and Wilson. Social secretary Kath Nickels did a superb job with variety nights, tramps suppers, lectures, dances and a multitude of other events.

1938: Formation of photographic section. Secretary TW Seager. Donington Park Rally. Leicestershire DA won the Jubilee Trophy,

1939 - 1945 : During the Second World War there was a strong determination to keep the DA going, although so many members were in the forces. Connie Seager looked after the clubroom and social events. Secretary Geoff Markham kept the committee together. Rides were held, as contributors to this book make clear.

1947: DA Golden Jubilee. Melton section formed. Jubilee dance at Foresters Institute and rally at Welham.

1951: Festival of Britain.Celebrated by a Festival of Cycling at Fort Dunlop. Anniversary feature in Mr Leicester's Diary of Leicester Mercury shows Rhona and Anita Williams with the banners for Hinckley section. Harold Williams, of Hinckley, working to keep paths open in the Bosworth Field area. Charnwood section formed.

The successful youth section, started in the Sixties. Sid Standard is kneeling (left)

Rhona and Anita Williams with the Hinckley banners

1952: Shepshed section formed and then merged with Loughborough section one year later.

1953: Coronation year: Eighteen members rode overnight to Harrogate for the CTC AGM and memorial unveiling. A DA camping section formed.

1955: First of 'Cyclists Special' rail excursions. Birmingham and Midland DA met the train at Worcester and led various paced and distance rides.

1957: DA Diamond Jubilee: Ride to retrace the original route to Wistow Park and Shearsby.

1960: London cyclists arrive at Great Central Station on a 'Cyclists' special to join runs led by Leicestershire DA members. DA members act as instructors for child cyclist proficiency schemes. Intermediates change of name to 'General's (now known as City).
Junior section formed very successfully by Sid Standard.

1962: DA form a racing offshoot - the Bradgate RC. In 1969 CTC membership was no longer required and so this club severed official links with the DA.

1972:. First AIT rally to be held in Britain lasting a week. Organised by Ken Pepper/Graham Preston Third Birthday Rides, but first outside Godalming, incorporated into above rally.

1978: CTC Centenary Year. Round Britain relay ride. Leicestershire leg Croxton Kerrial to Uppingham via Oakham. DA centenary float in Ashby carnival. All night ride to Harrogate. Centenary medals issued for standard rides. National Secretary, Les Warner MBE starts Leicestershire DA heat of the BCTC. National President Bill Oakley guest of honour at Charnwood section social.

1982: Loiterers and Photographic section make a decision to continue as a section, following the death of their secretary Alan (Buster)

Haywood. First town twinning visit to France by Charnwood member, Ron Johnson

1983: Sid Mottram, President for 13 years between 1960 - 76, died aged 75. Sid was a founder member of the Leicestershire Cyclists' Association and a well known Leicester cycle dealer. Lutterworth section formed. Charnwood section begin their long association with Romans sur Isere.

1984: DA organise the Birthday Rides based at Scraptoft College.

1985: Frank Holden, Founder member of Charnwood section, died on 31st August. Dave Cottle died while out with the Loughborough section on 3rd November.

1986: Triennial Veterans Rides; New Years Eve party - tramps supper; Tree planting ceremony in Shrewsbury; 'Thank you' gift to Janet and Tony Cooper, who recently moved from Copt Oak YH.

1987: 90th anniversary year. Ed Broom, DA secretary for five years 1958-1963 died aged 77; National Dinner held in Leicester on 21st February, organised by Phyllis Williams and Ron Johnson, 178 attended; President's Ride (Morgan Reynolds) also attended by National President Ivy Thorpe. John Allen wins BCTC final.

1988: New Years Eve (31.12.87) Fancy Dress party Theme 'A la Francais - Dress and food.

1989: Triennial Vets Rides. David Sulley, founder member of Lutterworth section, died 2nd April, aged 55, while taking part in the 100/50 mile standard rides. Ron Johnson and DA members help local charity, Menphys, in organising a sponsored ride around the cyclepaths of Leicester City and immediate area.

1990: Kim Suffolk wins BCTC final in Norfolk

1991: Charnwood Section celebrates 40 years with anniversary tea on

Great Central Railway train. Ray Clay - Loughborough Easy Rider - completes End to End in coldest, wettest June for 300 years.

1992: Vets Triennial Rides. Kim Suffolk second overall in DATC with Ben Keetley first junior and fourth overall.

1993: Ben Keetley again takes first junior in DATC. Eric Neal and Dennis Heggs complete End to End

1994: Countryside Challenge Weekend based at Botcheston. Saturday: map reading organised by Kim Suffolk followed by saddlebag sale and slide show organised by Ron Johnson; Sunday: All Terrain Ride organised by Ron Johnson. Family section started by Loughborough section members Ariadne Tampion and John Catt. Eileen Johnson, in her second year as President, was invited by Leicester City's lady Lord Mayor to join her and eight other lady cycle club officials to a lunch to welcome the riders in to the Leicestershire stage of the Kelloggs Tour of Britain. DATC: Lyn Stott first lady; Katie Keetley first junior; BCTC Peter Witting overall winner; Kim Suffolk second place; Lyn Stott first lady; Katie Keetley first junior girl.

1995: Triennial Rides: Kim Suffolk wins the DATC, Katie Keetley - first junior girl

1996: Morgan Reynolds completes End to End. Sustrans cyclepath network extended into Leicestershire. Kim Suffolk wins the DATC Katie Keetley - first junior girl (completes hat-trick).

1997: Centennial dinner and prize presentation, Belmont Hotel Leicester, February; Cycle '97 exhibition, City Rooms, Leicester. Co-produced with Leicester City Council and grant-aided by them in March; Bike Express trip to Provence in May; Birthday Rides in August.

The above short extracts will raise more questions than they answer. Why haven't they included so and so?. What on earth did they put that in for? All we can do is plead EOE. (Errors and Omissions excepted)

Never on a Sunday

by Kathleen Nickels

As it is the Centenary year of the Leicestershire and Rutland DA, our President and Bill Seager, have decided that I must be the person with the longest membership and so with the longest memories of old DA riders and personalities.

I joined the CTC in 1924 when I was 17 years old. I knew nothing about the CTC - just enjoyed riding about with any of the young apprentices at the engineering firm I worked for. I was also going to night school to sharpen up my shorthand and used to bike there, of course. One day, while I was putting my bike into the bike racks, another girl in my class, also sharpening up her shorthand, was racking her bike too. After a few weeks she asked me if I liked cycling. I said "Very much." She told me she was in the CTC who were a good crowd and asked if I would like to have a ride with them. Of course I immediately said "Yes" and so began many happy years of friendships.

It didn't get me a husband (I had already got him marked out among the apprentices) but I was willing to keep my eyes on the alert! In those days clubruns were on Saturday afternoons. Nobody in the British Isles would have dreamed of doing anything for pleasure on a Sunday. Church in the morning and Sunday school in the afternoon for young people were the only permissible occupations (strict parents would not allow any reading but the Bible). My nightschool friend, I still didn't know her name, or she mine, told me the meeting place was at a tram terminus (I have forgotten which) at 2-30pm. I was there promptly - and so began many happy experiences.

The people whose names I remember from that ride were: Fred Almond, 'Cigs' (that was his nickname) and Tom, their two sisters whose names, I am ashamed to say, I have forgotten; Dick Barnes and his sister Sis Barnes, Stanley (Stan) Kirk and his sister Kathleen Kirk, (my nightschool friend) Rupert Kirk (no relation), Lew Osborn, Charlie Fisher and his brother (whose name I can't remember) and Charlie Garner (who I think was the secretary).

We never went far in those days. The country roads were very rough and often there were water splashes (brooks running across the road) and in any case, we couldn't stay out late. We always had our tea in either farmhouses or public houses, and very good they were. Don't be alarmed at 'public houses.' You can't have any idea how quiet everywhere was in those days. I'll explain about the public houses: every village had its own cricket team and, of course, played the other villages on Saturday afternoons during the season. The home team entertained the visitors for tea, served when the first team to bat was all- out. And where else was big enough but the local pub, to house the local team, their followers and the visiting team and their followers? It was all most respectable, jolly and friendly. If the first batting team looked well stuck in, we had our tea first. If the bowlers were getting them out quickly, we had to wait while the cricketers had theirs. We didn't mind and we liked to watch the play. The farmhouses were lonely, set among fields well away from any road but again were happy and friendly places to have tea.

A good few years later, when we had a large number of riders, we began to get a bad reputation. There began to be a large number of males who could not resist picking up a football and kicking it about. And a village street or field was just the place for it. It got so bad at one time that we had a representative from Headquarters. After a lecture from him we all settled down again. The secretary, I won't mention his name, got out of all responsibility by saying he was taking a quiet walk in the local wood when this unannounced visit occurred. So much for clubruns at the weekend!

In the week, during the summer, we met on Wednesday nights and played tennis. We all used to meet at the Garner's, they lived near a park and the secretary booked us a court for the evening. We ran a competition and a very good time was had by all. I won't say anything about the quality of the tennis, but we all enjoyed it and that was all anyone cared about.

In the winter we had a clubroom. At that time in Leicester there was a chain of cafes named 'Winn's' situated round the centre of the town and we engaged a room in one of them each Wednesday in the winter months. I can't imagine how it paid them to have us. Of course in the evening they were closed for business, but we were allowed to play the piano and have a dance. We could only afford a cup of coffee, but the manageress and a waitress were there and they enjoyed it all as much as we did.

Those early days were so happy and simple. No courting, no sex appeal, no special friends, no upsets. Just a happy crowd of people. I must tell you one last thing: Dick Barnes rode a 'Rudge' which had a ten year guarantee and whenever anyone had a breakdown, how he rammed this guarantee home. But our day came, believe me. It was only two runs after Dick's guarantee expired that his frame broke. Was his face red - and was our laughter loud!

Gleanings from the Gazette

We know that the Leicestershire DA was formed over the years of 1896-97 and know the names of most of the people involved. What we do not know is the way that people thought in those days, although those thoughts were obviously very different from those of today. The report that 1/- subscription was taken from those joining outings indicates that only the relatively well off would have been able to take part.

The CTC Gazette gives some fascinating insights into the way things were. Over the period 1895-97 various controversies were being aired. Nationally the CTC was divided on whether a clubroom or clubhouse should be provided for members. One member wrote against the idea, pointing out "the CTC is an association, not a club. Members can communicate by correspondence in the Gazette, or can see and speak to each other at the various meetings that are held. Members are drawn from all classes of society, and I cannot imagine that there is any general anxiety to meet together socially."

This view was immediately refuted in the next edition by 'WOR.' in which he supports the idea of a clubroom or house "to further strengthen the club in enabling it to fulfil its aims. It is not necessary to be intimate with every man one meets in a clubhouse, whether he be of inferior rank or otherwise, and as long as a members' manners are not positively objectionable, his presence in a club are of no moment one way or the other."

A very lively debate took place in the letters' section concerning dress for ladies. Rational dress was considered by some to be immodest, as it was similar to clothes worn by men, i.e. a divided skirt or knickers.

In January 1896 'member 9761' wrote that he favoured rational dress on two grounds, firstly, as he often said to his wife, "If you rode like those women I could not accompany you." (This referred to the fact that skirts blew in the wind and ankles could be exposed). Secondly, the dress adopted as 'rational' was not a bit like men's clothing. They were not the slightest bit 'mannish' but thoroughly feminine - no man would wear these any more than a skirt and that the even distribution of the dress on each side of the machine was a distinct gain in appearance." He trusted that many lady members would adopt the costume cut full and of quiet colour for the coming season. (Leicester had an official ladies' and men's cycling tailor, F Brett, Peterborough House, Granby St.)

However, in the same edition, 'member 15617' was equally vehement that skirts should always be worn - she had ridden several hundred miles without ever having her skirt caught in the wheels or even by the pedals when 'flying hills.' She achieved this by having her skirt made of a fawn coloured covert coating, perfectly plain and narrower than an ordinary walking dress. The hem measured two and three-eighth yards and was faced inside four-inches deep, with thin brown leather. It was short walking length and cleared the ground by three-inches. To keep the skirt in its proper place, two bands of broad black silk elastic were buckled or sewn to the proper size for fitting around the legs just above the ankles. To these bands, straps four inches long, made of the same silk elastic, were sewn. Strong safety pins were attached to the other end of the strap and were then fastened to the inside of the skirt, four-inches above the hem and 12 - 15 inches from either side of the centre point. "By this arrangement the skirt never moves from its proper position, however windy the day may be, nor is there the slightest difficulty when mounting or dismounting."

Before we leave this fascinating topic we note that 'member 280' was also against rational dress on the grounds that "it is equally dangerous to enter the hunting field wearing a skirt, but sentiment demands that ladies' and gentlemen's clothes should be distinctively different and it surely cannot be wise to set this at naught?"

Another topic was whether or not bicycles should have brakes. They were generally felt to be unnecessary and indeed in some cases quite "dangerous." Mrs E Main wrote from St Moritz about the form of brake employed in Switzerland, which was "a spreading bough of a tree tied by a rope beneath the saddle and allowed to trail about a yard behind the machine."

She explained that during continuous descents of several miles, which occurred on Alpine passes, few riders cared to wear out tyres and shoe leather by applying their feet to the edge of the front tyre, while a heavy trailing branch restrained the machine to exactly the extent desired by the rider, was absolutely safe, easily attached and unproductive of the slightest injury to any part of the cycle." This lady also refers to her 'self healing air chambers' which had been fitted inside her Palmer Tyres.

She reported that, despite sharp stones on the road, she had no need to dismount and suffered no punctures. The only sign of wear was where small punctures could be seen. The subject of brakes was raised again following this letter, by Miss Erskine, writing for the Ladies Page. She described the branch as a useful suggestion, but wondered would it be "an awkward adjunct on roads on which there was much traffic." She said that she had not tried the pneumatic nor the hydraulic brake, but suggested that a trailing brake such as Singer used to fit to Challenge bicycles was satisfactory. She herself used a band brake on the hub of respectable diameter - actuated by the foot.

Advice concerning conduct in thunderstorms was detailed in Nov. 1895. "The rider should dismount, leave the bicycle and lie down flat in the middle of the road if shelter is unavailable." After this gem of advice we discover what took place during the first season of the Leicestershire DA. Early in 1897 the new committee agreed to seek the co-operation of the consuls by welcoming them into committee.

The first run took place on Saturday 19th March , going to Woodhouse Eaves via Quorndon followed by a Whitsun tour to Skegness on Saturday 28th May . And on Saturday 18th June a large group of members from Leicester, Nottingham and Loughborough met to visit Taylors' Bell Foundry. Mr JW Taylor and his son conducted them throughout the works, welcoming them warmly.

At a committee meeting on 13th May a scheme for providing dinners for roadmen was discussed and agreed. Eventually the first of these took place during June at Kegworth and Markfield, followed by further dinners at Coalville, Hallaton, Market Harborough, Melton Mowbray and Loughborough. We know that 46 attended at Loughborough, which was enjoyed by all. These meals were paid for by subscription from local CTC members.

By now arrangements had been agreed with the Midland Railway Co. for the adoption of tourist bookings from Leicester. No reports are available, but we must assume the members took advantage of this. At the October committee meeting the hon. solicitor, Mr F Armstrong, reported that he undertook to deal with several cases of refusal by innkeepers to supply tea and other refreshment to club members. (This would be considered to be a serious matter when the renewing of a licence came up before magistrates). The other hon. solicitor, Mr TJ Webb undertook to reply to a letter from the Rev LH Pearson concerning the illegal practice of strewing hedge cuttings about the highways.

The year drew to a close with a musical evening and lecture by Mr John Loseby "Cycle Touring Reminiscences" held in the Mayor's Parlour of the Town Hall on Thursday 15th December at 8 pm. All members and friends were cordially invited.

We now move on 20 years to 1917, during the First World War, to find that runs were held every Saturday at 3 pm and Sunday at 10am - on an impromptu basis. The meeting place was Welford Place. Lunch was carried on Sundays and the then secretary, Mr BL M'Quillan, reported in the Gazette that "liquid for internal irrigation" would be obtainable between 12 - 2.30 pm."

It was agreed at the annual meeting to publish a runs' programme if members would support them. And a proposal for joint runs with various cycling clubs in early May was agreed. A weekend run to Turvey (Beds) was organised for the 4th and 5th of May with an appeal to the members to support this and to recruit new members. In June an invitation went out to all local cyclists to join in a run to Charnwood Forest.

The committee in July decided, in deference to the ration regulations, that members should carry refreshments on all runs, and that all runs should start 15 mins after stated times. At the October committee they viewed "with dismay the proposal to amalgamate with the NCU and trust that the council will not countenance this as it would be disastrous to the Club." Following a motor cycle fatality on the Six Hills the attention of the county council was drawn to the dangerous state of this road.

In November the committee was told that "The Borough Surveyor with his usual kindness has given immediate attention to the holey state of London Road, and that surface repairs are now underway." The Chief Constable had agreed to attend to the matter of steel scrap on the road. One offender had already been warned of the consequences of allowing such material to fall from his cart. Following this meeting, the secretary Mr M'Quillan sent a report to the Gazette stating that "in compliance with the urgent need for economy" the committee had patriotically decided to save the 15 minutes formerly wasted on late comers, the runs henceforth to start promptly on time.

A report on the December committee meeting reveals that the proposed club and rest houses, proposed by a special national sub-committee, were discussed. It was agreed to support these, although the Leicestershire DA needed more information. The correspondence columns were still concerned with the dress lady cyclists' could properly wear. In March a "mere man" asks why ladies still cycled in skirts and suggested a gymnastic costume as a suitable alternative, although a lady writing in May reported that during a tour in France during 1913 she saw only one lady wearing ' Rational' costume whereas previously it had been a common sight.

It would seem that despite having been at war for three years, cycle tourists were still active. One 61 year old, who had first toured during the 1870s, was sorry not to have met any other cycle tourists on his recent tour through the Yorkshire Dales, Westmoreland, Cumberland, Northumberland and Durham. In April 'member 2567' was advertising several Gazettes for sale, with the proceeds to go to the NCU Prisoners of War Fund. In June this fund appealed for more money to maintain the weekly food parcels sent to our men imprisoned in Germany. Ladies could help by knitting socks, the wool for which would be forwarded upon application.

In May RG Pagets were again able to advertise their waterproof clothing. They regretted having had to discontinue their previous offer owing to the great demand for war materials, but were now able to supply from stock. Also in May, a member wrote to thank the CTC for the Gazette which brought 'good old Blighty' scenes up to the trenches. He said he was looking forward to the day when he would be riding along to the old haunts and thought all members would be eagerly awaiting the days of peace when he hoped to "carry on in the good old ways. (Eighty years on we cannot say whether or not he was able to achieve this).

Another jump in time to the 50th year celebrations which opened with the Loiterers Christmas party at Blakeshays Farm on 19th December 1946 when 80 members and friends enjoyed themselves, followed by a New Year party on 5th January 1947 when 20 members attended. The DA Dance at the Foresters' Institute on 27th February cost 2/- while Mr W Seagar had presented a lantern lecture on "The Emerald Isle" on 13th February.

An easy riders section was formed and the new Melton Mowbray section announced that members were very welcome. In July six DA members took part in the Leicester Forest CC 100 in 8. The Leicestershire/Rutland Rally took place at Welham in fine weather on 21st Sept. Members who wished to attend had to deposit 2/- with their section secretaries by 7th Sept.

A new hard riders section was being formed and a 100 in 8 hours was to be held on 12th October, with all entries required in advance by the section secretaries. Summer tours taken by members included The Hebrides, Eire and Southern and Northern France. There was a dance at the Forresters Institute on the 7th November followed by a social at the clubroom on the 22nd. Both cost 2/-.

The loiterers and Melton sections held a joint Guy Fawkes social while the intermediates enjoyed a week end away in Derbyshire. The year ended with the annual Christmas Social on 18th December at 7.45pm at the Forrester Institute (2/-).

Correspondence during 1947 started with a complaint from Mr TH Pettipher that "in face of the scarcity of paper, a whole page was devoted to a crossword puzzle", and 'EEG' pointed out that before the war many complained how frequently ham and eggs were served, whereas now mouths watered at the prospect, although caterers would not be allowed to serve them, even if they had any to serve.

In February there was much criticism of the editorial policy of giving too much space to personal recollections - more articles on touring by clubmen were requested - but WS Partington even pleaded "but don't give us Wayfarer or Oakley."

In March letters began to appear from tours abroad and the value of Esperanto was hotly debated with the pros and cons about equal. Wigan section began rides for blind stokers with four tandems. York Rally was attended by 10,000. There was a plea for manufacturers to produce a lightweight cycle. It came from a member with fond memories of the Dursley Pedersen of 40 years ago which weighed between 11 and 121bs. H Hunter then replied that the 531 superlight sold at £27.7/3d minus gadgets, while a sports model sold at £17, including front dyno hub and three-speed gear. He valued the gadgets at about £5, which meant a difference in price of £15. He asked whether 531 frames and Endrick light alloy rims were worth all that? JJ Cooper recommended the touring handbook be discontinued as they fell into the wrong hands (of non-members) which resulted in CTC appointments being crowded out by non-member motorists.

The vexed question of dress arose again with PC Taylor writing to complain about cyclists “riding half naked with sheath knives in their belts which bring all cyclists into disrepute.”

As we near the end of the century, with the Leicestershire DA preparing to celebrate its centenary, it is to find that cycling is once more high on the public agenda. The problems to be resolved during the years after 2000 on will be very different to those which faced our founders. Not many members will find it necessary to trail branches to help them stop, nor be prepared to lie down in the road during thunderstorms. Ladies can now wear what they find to be most comfortable, without attracting either advice or criticism. But cyclists are now barred from certain public roads which are designated motorways. They have to contend with ever larger and longer lorries, thundering by at high speed, and find that many of the junctions and roundabouts present problems, because the size and speed of vehicles commandeer priority. It is no longer easy to take a bicycle on a train, indeed trains no longer reach the parts our founders would have taken for granted. We do have the advantage of aeroplanes whisking us off to undreamed of destinations and we can even take our bicycles with us.

We can buy mountain bikes to take us through the many bridleways and green tracks which are still available, and there is a charity - Sustrans - devoted to providing cycle routes away from any traffic throughout the British Isles.

There is public debate on reducing the amount of motor traffic to reduce pollution. Unfortunately not enough is being done to encourage more people to cycle as a means of transport. Even cyclists are accustomed to putting their bikes in or on to cars to get more easily to different cycling events and areas. Our rights officers' work hard in conjunction with local councils to ensure that numerous road schemes are not creating more hazards for cyclists and it seems that more people are now prepared to take to two wheels for an enjoyable leisure pursuit.

We are confident that cycling will be an important part of the lives of people just as it has been in the past and the Leicestershire DA will be proud to continue into the future the work that has already been done in the past.

Testimonial to the benefits of cycling

The telegram read "Come at once - job waiting." That summoned Walter Clarke to Leicester in 1921. Walter had recently lost his job on the railway at Rugby, so he set out on his bicycle, in company with his 15 year old daughter, Florence, and took up the promised position at the gas works.

Florrie had worked for a short while at a 'bespoke' orthopedic shoe factory at Long Buckby but fancied her chances in the hosiery trade and very quickly obtained a position at Johnson and Barnes as a mender in their warehouse.

Ninety year old Florrie's blue eyes sparkled as she recalled her early days in Leicester and particularly the joys of cycling. Every Saturday she and her father would ride from Leicester to West Haddon (Northamptonshire) where she had been born. She would then go dancing with her friends and on Sundays she and Walter would cycle back to Leicester.

Before long the whole family was established in Leicester and in 1926, while convalescing from appendicitis, Florrie met Sydney Wilson. He walked her home from chapel and soon they began to go for cycle rides together.

In 1927 they ordered a tandem, a Freddie Grubb, from London. This was to be their pride and joy for many years.Florrie and Syd soon joined the Cyclists' Touring Club and belonged to the section called 'the Hard riders' who would frequently ride 100 miles on a Sunday, leaving from a tram terminus. The leader would have reconnoitred the route and pre-booked the tea. Those leaving early would leave a note at the terminus for later followers. A 'sweeper' would always set out last to round up any stragglers.

Florrie laughed as she recalled the clothes they wore for their rides. "Syd had a ginger tweed cycling suit, with plus fours, and always a waistcoat and collar and tie," she said. Asked how she had dressed to go cycling, "As inconspicuously as possible" she replied.

One particular Sunday someone out in front was showing a fine turn of speed when he missed a bend in the road, went straight through a hedge and into a duck pond. The rest of the cyclists arrived to see him emerging from the pond covered in weed. "His girl friend thought it most unfair that I took a photo of him," said Florrie. "She was very displeased with me."

A traditional cyclists' wedding. Florrie and Syd's happy day

In 1932, Florrie and Syd were married in King Richards Road Methodist Church. Syd had suggested that they ride to church on their solo bikes and return on the tandem, Florrie told me, "but the family wouldn't have that!" However, they left the church under a traditional arch of wheels. The honeymoon involved the beloved tandem, of course, which accompanied them on a train to Bristol from where they toured Devon and Cornwall.

When young Florence (always known as Eileen) was born, Florrie senior did not give up cycling. First they had a sidecar attached to the tandem, then Eileen perched between her parents. Finally, Florrie took to a solo bike again as Eileen occupied the back seat of the tandem.

Every weekend would see them cycling in Charnwood Forest and beyond. During the war holidays were spent with Mrs Bird in Matlock Bath. The luggage was taken in a large travelling trunk by Carter Patterson while Florrie, Syd and Eileen cycled all the way.

The other half of the tandem - Syd Wilson

Florrie and Syd certainly started a cycling dynasty. Her daughter Eileen and husband Ron (Johnson) have taken their bicycles all over the world, from France to New Zealand, USA to China. "Have bicycle will travel," seems to be their motto.

Grandson Michael accompanied the British mountain bike team to the Atlanta Olympics as manager of the mountain bike team, and great grandchildren, Claire and Antony regularly take to their bikes with Mum and Dad, Gail and John Bown.

That first bike ride to Leicester certainly started something and if you are looking for a testimonial to the benefits of cycling - just get Florrie to reminisce about those early days.

No one dared to pass the captain

Frank Coulson's memories of his long standing love of cycling include racing during the 1920s in addition to his CTC membership and activities. Frank was a schoolboy friend of Syd Wilson. They lived in adjoining streets in the Tudor Road area of Leicester and rode their bicycles everywhere, so when Frank started to work it was a foregone conclusion that he would travel there and back by bicycle. Earl Shilton was the destination, which gave him 22 miles of training each day and he slowly, but surely, became faster and fitter.

In 1923 a new clubroom was opened by the Leicestershire DA at the Turkey Cafe and a new group formed to ride on Thursday afternoons. This was necessary as not all mothers would allow their teenage sons and daughters to ride a bicycle on Sundays as the 'day of rest' was much more strictly observed at this time. This arrangement suited Frank very well, as by now he had begun working for JW Wales, a noted china and pottery supplier with a shop at the top of Leicester Market Place.

Another custom in this period was for shops to close for half a day every week and Thursday was Leicester's half day closing. Frank laughed as he recalled one particular Thursday run when the club rode out to Lubbenham for tea. On the return ride, as they paused in Market Harborough, they discovered that one of the party had left a jacket behind at the tea stop. Frank offered to ride back for it, but when he got there he discovered the leader had not paid for the teas!

There was nothing for it but to ride back to Market Harborough, collect the cash, then ride back to Lubbenham to hand it over. Then it was back to Market Harborough again - with the jacket - and then finally back to Leicester and home. Another very popular ride was on Thursday evenings to hear the Carillon play in Loughborough park. Their aim being to reach the top of Red Hill in Birstall within the half hour, which was considered to be good going.

The group would ride around 100 miles each time they had a full day out and new riders had to fend for themselves as they were 'burnt off' until they 'found their legs.' But the rule about not passing the leader was very strictly observed and if ever he shouted "Captain walking" on a steep hill, then everyone immediately dismounted and walked with him.

Tuesday evenings were spent riding to Dunton Bassett, where they met up with the Coventry section before riding back to their starting points. Friendly relations were enjoyed with all the adjoining DAs and Frank remembers being invited, with others, to Northampton's annual dinner one year. After a stop at Lamport for refreshment, they continued into Northampton where they enjoyed a good meal before returning to their homes in Leicester.

Frank had a friend, Joe Wain, whose mother kept a paper shop in Belgrave Road and whose grandmother took the family to Cleethorpes for a holiday one year. Joe and Frank could only visit them at the weekend. They set out to ride there on a Saturday night. Unfortunately, they ran out of oil for their lights on the way, so they slept in a haystack near Saxondale until it was light enough to continue the next day.

Saxondale also brought back memories of racing events held there. You could get a cup of tea for 4d from the wooden hut by the side of the road, which was especially welcome as events started very early in the morning and they had to ride to them. A rule stating that everyone must wear black was very strictly enforced and anyone presenting themselves to the timekeeper considered to be improperly dressed was not allowed to start. There were very few cars on the road in those days and the Six Hills was a little used road. The 'Gate Hangs Well' at Syston was another popular venue for events and here you were able to change in their shed. Dick and Connie Barnes were fellow members of both the CTC and the Leicestershire Road Club, together with someone always known as '91' - because he only ever rode a 91-inch gear.

In 1925, together with some other members, they decided to form a racing section of the CTC to be known as Charnwood Racing Club. Stan Kirk and Frankie Bott were two other members whose names spring to mind. Frank himself had also been a member of Leicester Forest CC (formerly the Keir Hardie Cycling Club) and also of the Leicestershire Road Club. In 1924 Frank won the fastest novice award in a 25 mile time trial, recording 1 hour 19 minutes 5 seconds. This had improved to 1-12-07 by 1925, good enough to give him a second handicap prize. Also in 1925 Frank rode just over two hundred miles in the 12 hour standard ride.

In 1928 it was the Golden Jubilee of the formation of the Cyclists Touring Club and Leicestershire played their part in the celebrations. A Jubilee Dance was held on 6th March and the DA also took part in the National Round Britain CTC Jubilee Relay Ride. Frank was not able to take an active part in this ride, but he recalled that the signatures of the mayors of Leicester and Loughborough were obtained by two teams of riders from the DA. The ride in this section took place on Tuesday 12th June from Stamford via Uppingham to the De Montfort Hall, Leicester. Despite torrential rain between Uppingham and Leicester and some severe problems with a tyre, the four men and one lady were a mere 11 minutes late reaching the De Montfort Hall. The following day five men formed the team which left Leicester just before 6.30 am to arrive at Loughborough 50 minutes later. After obtaining the mayor's signature the group continued to Shardlow where Derby DA took over.

By 1930 Frank had met Vera Webster, the future Mrs Coulson, and in that year they were both vice presidents of the DA. Frank had given Vera membership of the CTC as a birthday present some years earlier and they continued to ride together until the mid 1950s. Vera was forced to retire from active cycling due to arthritis in her hands.

However, there are many happy memories of their rides and holidays together, one of which was to the Isle of Wight on a Bank Holiday week-end. By this time Frank was managing a large successful stall on Leicester market for JW Wales, making it quite impossible to get away on a Saturday. So Vera cycled alone to Banbury where she got bed and breakfast in a CTC guest house. Frank rode down the next day to meet her and they were then able to continue their tour. Another occasion, he recalled, was when they made a 6 am start to arrive at Matlock in time to take breakfast at Mrs Barnes'. It snowed heavily that day and she very kindly dried their socks by the fire. They continued to ride around and finished by following a snow plough down the Via Gellia to join what is now the A6 into Derby. Here they stopped at a friend's house for a pancake snack. The lady foolishly asked if they would like some more and she spent most of the rest of the evening cooking pancakes for them all.

One New Year's Eve they all rode out to Mrs Harrison's at Newtown Linford, where they had a party until it was time to climb to the top of Old John to sing Old Lang Syne before cycling back to Leicester.

Frank and Vera's son Graham also remembers holidays and weekends devoted to bicycle activities when he was young, but he did not embrace it with the same enthusiasm as his father, who kept his love of this demanding pursuit throughout his long life.

Thanks for the memory

Janet Gabbitas, a very young 78 year old, is married to Sam and they both live in the same house they have shared since their marriage in November 1939. They are both life long supporters of cycling and the CTC, with Janet campaigning vigorously over the years to promote her CLIC (Cyclists' Local Information Centre) based at her home. She has always nurtured a hope that CLIC could become the clearing house for people requiring help or information connected with cycling.

Janet met Sam when they rode with the Loiterers, and she remembers singing the 1930s song "Thanks for the Memory" on their way down to London to attend the Cycle Show at Earls Court and then on in the evening to the RTTC Best All Rounder prize presentation at Wembley Stadium, where Bertram Mills of Mills Circus fame entered the arena on a bike.

Others with them were Shirley (Pop) Stanage and Lily, Arthur White and Norah, Albert Widdowson and Kath before any of them were married. They stayed overnight at the Regent Palace Hotel and put their shoes outside the bedroom door to be cleaned. Janet's were brown and white brogues like the Prince of Wales wore to meet Mrs Simpson.

On another occasion she remembers Kath and George Nickels dancing the Maxima; Kath looking quite lovely in black lace and George saying he knew he wasn't drunk when he could still say "I was sitting on an anatomical saddle" Lovely glimpses of a by-gone age which was soon to be over. The Second World War started in Sept 1939 and Janet and Sam married on November 4th of that year. They have lived in the same house on top of a 1 in 7 hill in Avebury Avenue, off Anstey Lane, Leicester ever since, renting it for 14s per week at first and eventually buying it for £620. They were originally offered it for £475, but by the time they had thought about it and considered their situation the price had risen.

During the war there was a weekly clubroom at the Foresters' Institute run by Kath Nickels and Lal Whitmore. Everyone helped with cakes and cheese sandwiches then they all stood around talking and smoking. They would have spelling bees and sometimes someone would arrange a tramps' supper. Janet recalls Norah Fox going out to get

Talking and smoking continue on their runs

some chips for one of these. At a 6d hop there would be a piano, violin and drums for dancing.

In 1944 their first daughter Hilary was born and so to continue cycling they bought the sidecar that Florrie and Syd Wilson had used for their daughter Eileen 10 years earlier. Hilary was followed in 1949 by Jean and in 1953 by Barbara. So yet another cycling family swelled the ranks of Leicestershire DA. There were so many young cycling families at this time that Ed and Betty Broom started a family section which prospered for many years.

Even after the war ended, most food was still rationed and in short supply. On one occasion, Hilary smeared the butter ration all over the sidecar cover. She would chew on a lump of suet, given to her by a kindly butcher, until it resembled lace.

Janet is a woman of strong religious belief, having tried various faiths, she is now a committed Catholic. But to her cycling is also close to a religion. As she puts it "Catholic faith for the mind, cycling for the body." She has very firm views on a variety of subjects, for example she has a horror of cycle paths which force riders into single file. "Jesus was looking for shepherds not sheep," she states firmly.

She has travelled to AIT rallies on many occasions with Ken Pepper. Poland, France and Holland being some that she mentioned.

Unfortunately Sam is now house bound suffering with arthritis and Janet suffered a breakdown which prevented her riding for some time. But after the tragic death of BB (Beryl Burton) on May Day Bank holiday Monday 1996, Janet decided she would rather die on her bike. She took herself off to 'Julies' to buy some shorts. The price of £30 came as something of a shock, after a lifetime of making her own from Crimplene. Now armed with a copy of Cycle Chat she feels that her opportunities are wide open.

The annual reunion of pre-war cyclists started by Janet Preston and Christine Smith for the Leicestershire Road Club, and now run by the same people for the Leicestershire Cyclists' Association, is very much enjoyed by Janet. She feels that Louis Armstrong was quite right when he sang:

The fields are green
The sky is blue
You have me and I have you
And I say to myself
What a wonderful world

She is of the opinion that cycling could save the world, provided it is done properly and responsibly through organisation and that people should join her in a CTC internet to create a "New Jerusalem in England's green and pleasant land."

A final plea from Janet: "Has anyone got a small lightweight tricycle for sale to start the 'Third Dimension Team?'

Sidecar became a family treasure

The story of a side-car begins in 1933 with the birth of a daughter to Florrie and Syd Wilson. As keen cyclists, it was not even contemplated that this event would curtail their trips out. After Eileen was born - in September - they began to look around and to economise so that as soon as they could find the right model, they would be able to go out as a complete family.

Eventually the Watsonian side-car was found and became a common sight in the streets in the West End of Leicester. Florrie and Syd had bought a house in Warwick Street, a comfortable three-bedroom terrace with access to the rear via an entry. The sidecar was fitted to the nearside of the tandem, which must have meant detaching it each time they returned from a run, as it was far too wide to get up the entry.

Unfortunately, Eileen cannot remember any actual runs in this gleaming coach-built beauty, although there are plenty of photographs recording the outfit. However, she can remember it with deep affection when it lived in the small third bedroom at 76 Warwick. (How difficult it must have been to manoeuvre it round the bend at the bottom of the stairs and then around the sharp bend at the top into the passage!) It was a large side-car built like the prow of a boat, with the front rising to a point, covered in some shiny hard material like pram panels. The inside was padded and it had a detachable seat across the width with the whole space in front empty, for legs or luggage whichever had the priority. When young Eileen wanted to sail away in her imagination, there was no need to have a box on the floor, she had her ready made Queen Mary upstairs.

As she grew older, she found it an excellent place to be when there were things to do, like setting tables for meals and even when it was time for the dreaded piano practice. It was a good place to curl up to read a book. And as the years passed, it became ever more necessary to curl, as by this time her legs would not fit into the front. To read she had to cram into the tiny space, with her knees somewhere near her ears.

Eileen's Uncle Stan married the sister of Sam Gabbitas (an old cycling friend of Florrie and Syd) and when Hilary was born to Sam and Janet in the austerity years during the war it was obvious that the side-car would find a new home. And so it proved. Janet and Sam bought it.

Eileen remembers it was like losing an old friend, although at 11 she could no longer cram herself into it. Even though she was fully mobile with a bicycle of her own it seemed like the end of an era.

Florrie Wilson with the celebrated Watsonian side-car

By the way, the entry by this time had become an extra cycle shed, there was Grandad Clarke's very large 'sit-up-and-beg' which had large quantities of fruit, flowers and vegetables tied to it on his return from his allotment. There was Florrie's sports model with straight bars, Syd's sports model with drop bars and Eileen's small wheel touring model. These were all ranged down the entry on the side of 76 (see picture). It was important to know this so that when visitors came in the dark they could shuffle down on the 74 side without barking their shins. In fact for many years after, even when the entry was clear, people in the know would walk crabwise down on the side of 74. If your bike was at the wrong end of the entry when you wanted to go out, the technique was a quick flick of the wrist which brought the bike on to its back wheel - then it was easy to push by the other cycles. But you had to be very careful not to damage the rear mudguard. Of course, if you were the last in, you needed to push all the others back a space in order to get in.

Janet and Sam cannot now remember who bought the side-car from them and so its whereabouts is a mystery. If you should discover it lying abandoned and forgotten in some bike shed from the past, please give it a friendly pat. Or better still tell Eileen.

Bill and Connie in tandem

One snowy day in February 1996, Connie and Bill Seager made us very welcome at their home in South Knighton Road, Leicester. From the moment Bill opened the door on bicycles hanging in the passage and propped against the wall, his interest in cycling was obvious. "Come in, come in" he said, ushering us into a warm and cosy living room where photos, cartoons and mementoes testified to the importance of cycling in the Seagers' lives.

With an energy that belies their years, (they are both in their eighties), Connie and Bill began to talk of their early days with the CTC and in particular the photographic section, started in 1938. It was a sort of double act with "Do you remember?" and "tell about ..." coming thick and fast.

Bill and Connie were both born in the village of Ibstock a year apart. They were, Bill confided, "Childhood sweethearts and jumped the brooks together." When Bill started work he used to cycle the 24 mile round trip to Leicester every day, but Connie did not start cycling until they bought a small double gent's tandem, in 1933 - a year after their marriage. Bill's cycling expertise had been honed over many years and in particular he perfected a running dismount which was frequently to land Connie in trouble. On one occasion in Derbyshire, as they came down a hill to a sharp bend, the front wheel hit the grass verge. "Jump" shouted Bill in his usual fashion, but Connie ended up in a clump of stinging nettles.

Another time, when going to the Goose Fair in Nottingham, the wheel went into a tram rut, Bill managed to leap off but poor Connie, who had strapped the pedals to her feet, was left lying in the road, feet in the air, with the tandem over her head, much to the amusement of a crowd which had gathered. Happily she was not hurt and in fact continued to ride until forced to give up by the onset of arthritis many years later.

Connie obviously learned a thing or two, because when a car forced Bill to turn at the traffic lights at Waterloo Street and Regent Road, this time she did jump off at Bill's command and the tandem was left trundling down the road on its own.

In 1933, when Bill joined the CTC, there were eight sections in Leicester and three sub-sections, which included the Thursday section and the camping club. In 1938 the photographic section was formed

In February 1938 the photographic section rode to Gaddesby. They are (back row left to right): A Smith, A Harris, W Seager, A Gnaegni; (front row): I Hall, Mrs A Gnaegni, Miss Smart, Mrs Seager and I Maples

and the first run took place on 6th February of that year to Gaddesby, nine members attending - Bill and Connie, Mr and Mrs Gnaegni, A Harris, Miss Lily Smart, H Smith, Ivor Hall, I Maples

Bill produced a dark blue album with the runs lovingly described and details of camera settings meticulously noted. It would appear that dashing plus fours were very much the order of the day. The photographic runs took place once a month and continue to this day. The Loiterers and Photographic section is now the oldest section in the District Association.

Although not listed on the first run, the name of Eric Neal is prominent from the second run. He was known as 'The Prof' because, no matter what the subject was, he knew all about it. Another member was known as "The Beast" because whatever happened he would remark "Oh its a beast." 'Willie Woodpecker' was so called because he had wooden heels for his shoes. 'Lamphole Lenny' gained his nickname when he cut a hole in the front of his waterproof cape to let his lamp shine through and "Tear arse Ted" was always off the front.

"Getting out of a warm bed and into the cold air at 4.30 am is nothing to be cheerful about. But most of the members of the photographic section must have had happy thoughts and good alarm clocks for 5 am saw them at the Humberstone Terminus ready for a ride to Wansford to see the Oaks Tandem Race." So begins an account of a full day on 17th July 1938.

After they had watched the race and done some lizard hunting and bird watching, the group of 14 made their way through Wing to Ridlington Manor House, where they all pursued a small boy and his pet pig Percy to get some excellent photographs.

Social events were very important in the 30s. Amongst their recollections Bill and Connie recalled the 'Loiterers' Hock' Leicestershire's answer to the Dunmow Flitch. Instead of proving that no cross word had passed between them during the year, the Hock was awarded for a poem showing why a married couple deserved to win.

Bill's poem started:

> *"I am the village blacksmith, big and strong*
> *Round here they all call me King Kong".*

However it may have continued, Bill and Connie won the hock, which the Chairman threw at them. Another episode they remembered with amusement was a 'Tramps' Supper' held in the social club in Nicholas Street. One diner seemed to be entering rather too much into the spirit of things, grabbing food off plates and swigging any drink in sight. "What section of the CTC are you in?" enquired one of the tramps. "I ain't in any of them buggers," he replied. He was in fact a real tramp! Bill also recalled bicycle polo in Victoria Park and a bicycle version of the Hallaton bottle kicking, from which he suffered some very painful bruises.

Percy the pig was a good subject for photographers

When the war started in 1939, people who remained in the area continued to cycle on their regular runs, often joined by folk stationed in the area. Bill volunteered for the RAF in 1942. He had hoped to get into photo reconnaissance, but after passing six tests successfully, he was asked two final questions: "What is 66 per cent of five square inches , and what fixer was used in 1846?" Because he did not know, he was turned down and eventually went into the RAF Regiment. He was stationed first at Dover, where the authorities found out that he did hairdressing and he became squadron barber. The squadron was guarding radar stations on the coast and Bill spent time cycling round the lanes first of Kent and later Devon. "I used to spin it out," he said "and sometimes took all day to cycle 20 miles."

While Bill was away, Connie continued to ride, but had only ever ridden a tandem so she needed someone to ride on the front. Various friends and acquaintances took her out , including some from the Pay Corps, billeted in the area. "I didn't know that," said Bill.

One of the favourite places for cyclists to go was Blakeshay Farm, in Newtown Linford. During the thirties, when riding in the Charnwood Forest, Bill had seen a sign 'teas.' The proprietor, Mrs Neale, was not particularly keen to serve cyclists, but was persuaded, and for many years this became a favourite tea stop. One Christmas during the war it was decided to have a party at the farm. There was a 'girls dormitory' and a 'boys dormitory.' Bill came home unexpectedly and the Neales gave up their room to them. Connie maintains that their only son Arthur is a 'Blakeshay baby!'

In the late forties, Bill began to take small groups abroad, Connie did not go with him. In those far off days there was a limit on the amount of money that could be taken abroad. It was amazing how far you could go on £25. Although Bill said he had never fired a gun "in anger" during the war, on his trips to France and Spain he had a gun pointed at him three times. One one occasion he was having a picnic at the side of a railway when two policemen came and demanded his papers at gunpoint. It was only afterwards that he learned that the Drummond family had been murdered in the vicinity and 'cyclists' were supposed to have been seen near the campsite.

Bill recalled how on a mountain pass in Spain he had a buckled wheel. In the village they found a man who built the wheel up then sat at the kerb side and tapped the rim to the correct shape and put the spokes back. He had no English and Bill had no Spanish, but as Bill says "You can go a long way with sign language." The charge for this service was approximately 2/-. "I gave him double," said Bill.

When Bill was abroad, Connie too was travelling, but only as far as Derbyshire. She recalls how she and son Arthur used to buy a 3/6d dog ticket to take the bikes on the train to Matlock. So, complete with Primus stoves, tea and sandwiches, they had some grand times. By this time she had learned to ride a solo machine.

She told how she and Arthur and her friend Lily and daughter stayed at the Charles Cotton Hotel at Hartington, where they had two rooms, dinner, bed and breakfast for two nights for the grand total of one guinea (£1.05). They went to the Charles Cotton for many years and when they arrived a maid would bring out tea and cakes.

Connie also has a very clear memory of one wet ride to Markfield. There were quite a few tandems out as well as solos. When they arrived it was to find that it wasn't possible to have the tea they had booked due to illness and so Bill invited everyone back to their home for tea! They quickly lit a fire in the front room, put the electric fire on in the other room and then lit the gas on the grill in the kitchen. Everyone had a little space in which to get warm and dry as best they could. Connie rushed out to buy a pound of butter, bread and some eggs and then provided everyone with poached eggs on toast, followed by tinned fruit and evaporated milk. Everything was then washed down with a good strong cup of tea.. Due to the pressure of space, George Nickels had an unfortunate accident which upended his poached egg and toast on to his knees, thus leading to the Seager saying when plates get near the edge of the table "Watch out you don't do a George Nickels."

Hospitality at the Seagers' home continues to this day. Connie pressed sandwiches and cakes on us when we visited them, but we avoided "doing a George Nickels."

A feeding station at the Oaks tandem race

Days out in 1938

From the 1938 runs book of the Photographic and Loiterers section, runs leader, Eric Neal writes:

The bridle path joining Barton in the Beans with Shackerstone is a pleasant track for the unhurried cyclist. Unannounced by any sign-post it appears to be unused even by the local people. The small gates are thickly overgrown with grass and weeds, while our passage through one field on this Sunday morning was impeded by growing wheat standing across the field.

The gloomy weather continually threatened rain and was heavy upon the spirits of those who wished to use their cameras, but improved as the day progressed. Our field path ended on the outskirts of Shackerstone village in a hard-baked mass of cow trodden mud, passing beneath the railway and over a bridge of the Ashby de la Zouch canal. We took the liberty of using the canal bank, some preferred to walk the three miles or so beside the water but much excitement was to be gained by riding between an aggressive hedge and a placid (but doubtlessly very wet) canal, with only a foot wide track in which to dodge bait-tins and fishing rods. Their owners chose between taking cover in the hedge bottom or clinging to the reeds at the water's edge. In that short stretch we passed at least 40 or 50 anglers and anglers' mates, showing the popularity of an idling pastime.

We dodged the anglers on our side of the canal, while the water reflected their friends across and behind them, the countryside changing from open fields to the thick spinney which fringes Gopsall Park. At one little bridge a pair of swans presented themselves for our photographers, their fee being a succession of titbits handed out by the girls.

The girls nearly joined the swans in the water but we were cheated of the snaps that the splash would have provided. A little further along we passed a small cottage where our secretary, who is a "local" to these parts, recalled that on one dark night he rode into the water here and had to receive assistance from the woman whose performance before her bedroom window had been the cause of his wetting.

From the canal to Appleby Magna is a short stretch, but our cafe proved to be one of those elusive places well outside the village which caused us to be late dining. Among the friends who joined us at lunch we were pleased to welcome Mr Jack Williams who had come to inspect the youngsters' progress. 'Old Jack's' accounts of his experiences during

Swans present themselves for the photographers

his 30 years of contributing photos to the Daily Sketch have often enlivened club conversation.

The tyre-bogey visited Mr Williams after lunch and we pulled his leg for some time, meanwhile we hatched a nefarious plot to cut the retailer out of the photochemical trade.

A suggestion that we should counter the dull day and not very interesting country by a visit to Tamworth Castle was quashed by riders who saw nothing 'functional' in the prospect, so a toddle round the countryside with the sun and cloud (and no more photographs) brought us by highway and field path to Sibson for tea. Puncture mending prevented several members reaching there until about six o'clock. The weather behaved itself most of the way home, but we finished up in our capes."

Tiptoe through the cornfield ...on the 1938 run

Psssst...... Does a spy wear a long black coat and a hat pulled down over his eyes, or does he blend in with a cycling party from the Photographic and Loiterers section, in baggy shorts with a camera at the ready?

In September 1938 on a ride to Repton Shrubs, the group was approached by a couple who said they had ridden over from Coventry with the express purpose of joining up with the section. The gentleman of the party, Mr X, we shall call him, appeared very knowledgeable about cameras and photography. When questioned about his own camera he said it had cost £13, but out of his lady friend's hearing, confessed to £19 - he hadn't wanted her to know how much he'd spent!

By 1938, of course, Hitler was already building his 'Third Reich which would last for a thousand years.' The German Intelligence services would have been anxious for details of airfields and factories in the Midlands. Were these just two innocents on a day out and was it just by chance that the Police were keeping a look out for the party in Repton? Alas, after all these years we'll never know - but it makes you wonder.

Police were on the lookout in Repton

Halcyon days of the 'nut and bolt' section

by Joyce Hames

Congratulations to the Leicestershire DA on a wonderful achievement. Arthur and I could not let this occasion go by without saying a very special 'Thank you' to the DA for the important role it has played in our lives.

We met in the old 'Inters' - often nick-named the 'nut and bolt section' of which Arthur was the then 'Hon.Sec.' - and married in 1951. We shall never forget those halcyon days in the 40s and 50s, when, with so many old friends, we explored the largely traffic-free highways and byways of our beautiful county and beyond.

When the next generation came along, the obvious thing was to form a family section. This got off the ground at a special social evening, held at the home of Eileen and Derek Blasdale. The section ran very successfully for 10 years or more. It was interesting to see the variety of methods there were for carrying the youngsters. The most popular was the kiddy-seat over the rear wheel (which we had for our son Alan) but new ideas were always being tried out. The side-car of my young days had given way to such things at the Rann Trailer. Ah - happy days, cementing life-long friendships!

However, my awareness of the DA goes back much further than this. I suppose it all started way back during First World War, with my father, Arthur Mabbutt and his old school pal Dick Barnes. Then in their teens, they 'mackled' together their first bikes from scrounged parts. It wasn't long before they had joined the DA and a new world opened up for them. Bowling along the mostly gravel-surfaced roads of those days, in the company of such cycling stalwarts as FCW Stevenson and Bernard M'Quillan was a revelation to them. They also received much encouragement and advice from their older colleagues.

Dad never tired of his love of the great outdoors, or of his fascination for map-reading, and this eventually rubbed off onto me. He had met my mother, Hettie Culverwell, in the early 20's when her brother Harry, who also rode with the DA, had taken him home to tea. However, before the romance could develop, it was essential that she should learn how to ride a bike - cycling having become an obsession with Dad by then. Obviously she did, for they were married in 1926 and set off for their short honeymoon in Warwickshire on a 'bicycle made for two.'

So that's how you do it... 'Uncle' Ed Broom shows the boys how to mend a puncture

Everything wasn't always sweetness and light though, as one touring incident was to prove. After doing some shopping at a village store, Dad set off thinking Mum was behind him on the tandem. For about two miles he chatted away, but became increasingly annoyed at the lack of response. Yes, you've guessed it - he'd left her behind and had to retrace his tracks to find her. Can't you just imagine her comments - not to mention the expression on her face when he re-appeared!

I first saw the light of day in May 1930 and my initiation into cycling began some six weeks later - in a sidecar. As the years went on we were out cycling most weekends, though not always with the club. I can just recall Welsh tours, and frequent trips into adjoining counties. Sadly by the time I was eleven, my mother started to suffer from arthritis and cycled less and less.

For several summers Dad and I went away on tours together. I can vividly remember one very wet and windy holiday in Devon in 1946. Accommodation and food was still scarce so soon after the Second World War, and I can remember going off down the main street in Barnstaple to buy some bread and cakes, carefully clutching our ration books. I had left Dad sheltering in a pub gateway, repairing a tear in his cape.

A group of riders in April 1921 on the lawn at the White Lion, Church Lawford, half an hour before sunset. Dick Barnes is second from the left, on the back row, and Arthur Mabbut is first from the left (seated)

How about this for the fashion of the day? Doesn't my mother look the 'Cat's Whiskers' in her 'Rationals'

He'd hung it over a door-latch to work on it. When I returned (full of the news that I'd nearly been hit by some falling guttering brought down by the gale force wind) he was hopping mad. Never had I heard such language! He'd stitched the back to the front and had to start all over again.

I think this holiday, coupled with the fact that my Mum was becoming more crippled, was the real finish of his cycling career, although his fascinating log-books, which I still have, record a couple more solo tours. Soon after this he bought an autobike and later, a motorbike.

So another era was about to begin. Dad said to me one day 'If you still want to cycle you'll have to 'paddle your own canoe' - a mixed metaphor if ever there was one. He suggested I join the CTC and shortly afterwards I was a regular rider with the Loiterers' Section. However, I was soon looking for younger company (they all seemed old enough to be my parents) and started going out with the newly-formed 'Generals' - a mad lot on reflection.

That was until one particular Sunday in July 1947. We were in a bunch nearing the brow of a hill near Twyford when an on-coming car ploughed into us. Trust me to be the one who landed up in the LRI with concussion and a fractured skull. Fortunately, as you will have gathered, this didn't deter me from pushing the pedals round for quite a few more happy years.

All our best wishes to the Leicestershire DA.

Here I am at the age of eight -- 'stoker' on the old faithful Saxon tandem

Hooked by a 93 mile ride

by Adele Heafield

Adele Heafield was a member of the WAAF during the Second World War and was posted to a camp in Cheshire, here she met and made friends with Mary Jackson from Bradford. It was to have a far reaching effect, as Adele goes on to explain.

Mary was a member of the Bradford General section of the CTC from before the war and had kept up her membership when we met in 1942. At first we had heavy service bikes, as ours was a 'dispersed unit' although later we were able to have our own cycles on camp and went for rides into the Cheshire countryside.

On one Whit Sunday we were off duty and Mary announced she was going to cycle to Dovedale. I asked if I could go too, but Mary said 'You'd never do it.' However I persisted until Mary agreed and lent me some khaki drill shorts (no double seat!) and we set off from camp which was at Cheadle Hulme near Stockport. My steed was a Raleigh 'Sports model' - no variable gears - and Mary rode a Baines 'Gate.' The route, via Macclesfield, Leek and Ashbourne was pretty hard going for me. We reached the lower end of Dovedale, then pushed our bikes as far as Milldale where we left the dale and plodded up the steep hill, in scorching heat, to join the Ashbourne - Buxton road.

We proceeded to Buxton, then one last climb and it was 'all down hill.' to Whaley Bridge and back to camp. If I recall correctly we did 93 miles that day and I was finally accepted by Mary as having possibilities as a cyclist. Mary was also a member of the YHA and so I joined that organisation as well as the CTC. We planned a little tour of Cornwall, and as members of the WAAF we were lucky to obtain travel warrants from Manchester to Padstow! So we only paid for the bikes on the train.

What a journey - Manchester to Plymouth - leaving at about midnight on a packed train, with only one seat between us the whole way. Then when we finally arrived, it was raining. We could scarcely believe it - the travel film we had seen at the local cinema showed only sunshine, blue skies and white clouds, although only in black and white of course! It was on this holiday that I had my first and last experience of riding 'fixed.' On the way back from Falmouth my freewheel gave up the ghost, fortunately Mary managed to tow me for some miles back to the hostel. The next morning she put it into the 'fixed' position and we set off to find the nearest garage. At the first crossroads I tried to stop pedalling with the inevitable result, I was soon rolling in the road!. However we walked to the next small garage where the owner offered to go into town and get the necessary parts. We left the bikes with him and went into Mevagissey on the local bus, collecting the bikes at the end of the day. This experience didn't put me off cycling, just off riding 'fixed'. We enjoyed Cornwall, but were unable to visit any of the beaches as they were still mined and sealed off by Danert wiring.

On release from the WAAF I found that my nearest section was Burton on Trent. I think it was the thought of the climb up Ashby Road at the end of a Sunday run - but I never did get around to going out with them. However, as a member of the CTC, I received the Gazette which contained an item about a proposed section to be formed in the Coalville/Ashby area. I contacted Phil Allen as requested and the rest as they say 'is history.'

Mary and I continued to spend every Bank Holiday weekend, apart from Christmas, youth hostelling. Following a very wet two week holiday in the North West of Scotland, we transferred our annual two week tour to Ireland. We cycled to Liverpool to catch the night boat to Dublin each year for about fifteen years. During this time we explored almost the whole country, apart from the extreme north of Co. Donegal, having enough memorable experiences to write a book.

Just think - if fate had not thrown Mary and me together in that Nissen hut in 1942 I could have missed out on all the years of fun, comradeship and many good friends that the CTC has given to me.

A glimpse into my cycling life

by Mary Margoschis

So the Leicestershire DA is 100 years old. I too feel I'm nearly there sometimes. I've been asked to 'look back.' Sorry, I cannot quite manage that far - but how about 60 years! That will take me to 1936-37.

It must have been about that era that my brother, two years my senior was cycling with the Shropshire DA northern section, fondly known as 'The Northern Lights.' How I would have loved to have gone along on some of those rides. But eventually I was allowed to accompany him in the summer holidays when I was home from school.

Being near the Welsh border, we had very beautiful country to cycle in. One favourite run was over the Berwyn mountains from Glyn Ceiriog to Plas Manta. The Alt-y-badi crossing. I well remember the start in Glyn Ceiriog. The lane went around the church and one was soon at the top or even looking down on the church, a 1 in 4, or thereabouts!

Llangollen was another good lunch and tea place, with a nice bit of country to ride over between meals and one of these was known as 'The Conquering Hero' I never managed it with the club, but I had one very memorable weekend with them. There was a house called Twyr-y-maen. (translated - Heap of Stones) somewhere in the Arrans or Arrings where lived two brothers and a sister, only one of whom could speak English. I believe two lady club members once became lost in the area and were helped, or perhaps I should say rescued, by this family and periodically the club would revisit. This required a letter sent sometime in advance of the planned visit, as the family would only collect any post at unknown times - an overnight stay also had to be arranged.

I must have pleaded successfully with my parents to be allowed to go on such an adventure. The Saturday night was spent at a small hotel near Bala. On arrival I was warned to take care and look into the 'chamber pot' should I wish to use it, as it had been known for 'The Lads' to pop in a piece of carbide, which would give rather dramatic results!

Sunday saw us up in the mountains, our cycles were left on a bank and we walked over the top to look down on the cottage. One of our members kindly took me ahead of the others and informed me that there was one other way we could arrive, by walking up a valley. He was certain one of the brothers would be out watching for us and on glimpsing us, he would re-enter the house, stoke the peat fire and I would see smoke come up the chimney. We came over the top and there I saw this little isolated cottage with dark brown patches here and there around where the peat had been cut. True to my friend's forecast, there stood a lone figure. We halted and waited for him to turn our way. We all waved at each other, then our host went in and a few moments after, smoke came up the chimney. By the time we made the last descent and entered the cottage, the very large black kettle was hanging on a spit over glowing heat and singing happily. I felt just as happy as that kettle sounded. After lunch in that friendly atmosphere we had a long ride home.

In 1941 I had a wartime touring holiday in the Lampeter- Llandovery area. The party consisted of my brother and his friend Rob, with me on the back of my brother's tandem. The area of wilderness down there seemed far greater than in our beloved North Wales. Our outings were tough, one taking us across what is now the Towey Forest and Lynn Brianne, east to west from Beulah to Tregaron. The longest was from Landovery, crossing our earlier route and going on north and a little west to Strata Florida, then out onto tarmac road at Pontrhyd fell to finish at the Post Office at Devil's Bridge.

By 1942 I had become a student nurse in Wolverhampton and my brother was in the Army. There was little time for cycling for pleasure. My bicycle was used to get me home for my days off - that must have been 30 or 40 miles. Sometimes I would leave after a day's duty to try not to miss any free time. We did have double summer time that gave us light evenings, but can anyone remember the 'top hat' light protectors we had to use so that Jerry could not see us. They also meant we could not see where we were going, or even each other.

Still at the back of my mind was that 'Conquering Hero Crossing'. The disappointment of not having done it must have been great, but why regrets. I thought, why not get on and have a go. Well it must have been the following summer when an opportunity arose.

There was an empty house at Shawbury, my brother in the Army, Mother away and a tandem hanging up in the garage. I tentatively approached a friend and fellow student who had the same days off as myself (we only had two and a half days per calendar month). Would she care to come home with me, as I would love to take her on a cycle ride? My brother's tandem was available.

Our days off commenced at 2 pm so we set off by train and bus to Shawbury. There was lots to do that evening. Tandem to get ready, food to prepare, cycle gear to find for Betty. I remember the last item was a rather old cape that figured prominently towards the end of our adventure. We must have managed a good start. I had never taken the front of the tandem before, but we made Llangollen for lunch. Then came the real challenge. Crossing the river we took the lane towards Carrog by the River Dee. On the right is the public house called "The Conquering Hero" with a track that brings one out on the top of the Horseshoe Pass. My memory is of dragging that machine over heather and bilberries, but all was well in the end, and we came out at the top of the hill - but in rain. We donned our rain wear and set off down to visit Valle Crucis Abbey and back to Llangollen, but the pressure of the wind in Betty's old cape was just too much and it rent in two.

Our journey home was uneventful. The next day was spent replacing all our borrowed items and two very tired students returning to duty. Amazingly, Betty and I remained good friends for the full period of our student days and at reunions for several more years were able to smile about how we had once spent our 'days off together in Wales. Looking back the actual crossing is insignificant in comparison to those I did in '41 with Richard and Rob, but for myself, having achieved it I was 'A conquering hero.'

My cycling days became less. I moved to Yorkshire where I had some pleasant weekends on my own in the Skipton area and managed one weekend from Leeds, where I now worked to the coast at Scarborough, Ravenscar and Robin Hood Bay. Then in 1952 my move to Birmingham saw an end to it. I no longer had a bicycle, but in 1978 when I moved to Norton Juxta Twycross I felt the country area called for me to try and start again. I bought a cycle from a warehouse and tried it out. Measham seemed reasonable. The wind was against me as I came home along Shelford Lane. I think I walked most of that lane. My bike spent more time in the garage than out. I was still working so did not have a great deal of time to 'get in trim.' By 1981 I was retired. I needed to take up some activity. I liked the town of Ashby and enrolled at night school for woodwork. This had long been a hobby of mine and through the school I was introduced to The Ashby Hill Walkers.

That walk on the second Sunday in the month was a life line to me for the next four or five years while I was caring for my mother, now well into her 90s. Then I met the walkers of the Charnwood section. I was invited to join them on their coach rambles. How I enjoyed their company. I made so many new friends.

Easter 94 was really the turning point. Alex had accompanied me on a cycle ride on a Thursday some five to six years before this, and I returned home amnesiac. I put this down to trying too hard to cycle up the hill in Polesworth so it was with great trepidation I inquired "Would I be a problem to the party going to Leek for Easter" Looking back now I think I felt a little bit 'left out' rather reminiscent of my 'Conquering Hero' experience. I was assured I would be welcome. A phone call to the farm brought permission to camp in my van and join the others for evening dinner. I was launched on a new cycling career, but what a launch!

The first day out I had a puncture before we even made Leek. After lunch I had a broken chain that was mended by Howard, while two of us held a cape over him to protect him from the snow. Several miles before the end of our ride I had a second puncture so I arrived back at the farm with my cycle in Howard's van. Next day the snow was so bad we all six piled into my van and had a day at Jodrell Bank. The question now was, would I make it?

Meriden Sunday, once again I ask "would I be a handicap if I came along?" By 8 am I was at Twycross in the pouring rain. I believe it was said by one of my friends "That will be the last we shall see of Mary after such a wet day as this" but no, I wanted to press on, especially after I heard about the Birthday Rides. This sounded a good holiday prospect to me. Howard and Betty gave me new hope of success by lending me a really nice bicycle for a year. I tried to get out around the lanes every day. I did my shopping in Ashby, Tamworth and Atherstone all 'on my bike', but always taking care not to try too hard to pedal up the steep hills. That lost Thursday still comes to mind on odd occasions.

Well it all paid off. I made the '94 Birthday rides and followed with '95 and '96. I enjoy my rides with the club. I hope the members out a few weeks ago enjoyed the ride I was down to lead? As I said to John Allen some time ago now, rejoining the CTC after some 50 years is one of the best moves I ever made. May we all have many more happy days out 'on two wheels.'

Luggage allowances were stingy

The Williams cycling family of Earl Shilton have many vivid memories of the years they rode together as part of the Hinckley section during the late 1940s and early 1950s. Harold rode tandem with daughter Anita as stoker while older sister Rhona rode solo.

John their younger brother remembers that young riders did not expect to have new bicycles until they began earning and even then they were usually in their late teens by the time they had accumulated enough. He also recalls that most bicycles at that time were masterpieces of ingenuity, bits were modified from other bits and 'make do and mend' was the only way to keep a bike on the road.

Punctures were repaired using old inner tubes cut up and stuck on with adhesive, acquired from the shoe factory down the road. All bike sheds smelt of neatsfoot oil, this was used to keep leather Brooks saddles in good condition, although this resulted in stained patches on shorts and trousers.

Harold was for many years secretary of Hinckley section and it was he who helped organise the first DA carol service in 1952. This was at Stapleton church and now, 45 unbroken years later, has visited every area of Leicestershire becoming a very important date in the local cycling calendar.

Holidays were opportunities to visit other areas. The Lake District, Southern Scotland and Wales were favourite. Anita once stoked the tandem to Barmouth when it rained all the way there. She claims that she pushed her father most of the way, and this proved good training for when she rode a solo and was easily able to keep up with the section, although Harold had thought it unlikely. Both Rhona and Anita recollect how strict Harold was in limiting their luggage when on tour - one piece of soap and one comb between them, one pair of shorts and one jacket each and no trousers - even on Easter tours when it could be bitterly cold.

They wore ex Land Army shorts with very wide legs which could prove very draughty. On one occasion they were invited to help with the milking at Mr and Mrs Banks' farm which was a CTC accommodation in the Cat and Fiddle area. When the time came, early in the morning, Rhona, being the elder sister, snuggled back down into bed but sent Anita to keep their promise to help. It was a very cold start to that day's cycling. When they met some friends who had included in their luggage a light cotton skirt to wear in the evenings, the two sisters decided to take matters into their own hands. Once they had received their holiday money from work, they took the rest of the day off to visit C and A where they bought attractive shorts and clothes for their forthcoming holidays. They particularly enjoyed their new close fitting shorts.

Youth hostelling was a popular way of spending weekends and holidays away. Dimmingsdale was a collection of chicken huts, with washrooms that had only cold water and enamel basins. On their first visit they chose the wrong hut for their early morning wash and were only just dressed when the men arrived for their shave. During this trip they investigated a hole in a hedge and found themselves in the grounds of Alton Towers. This had very recently been vacated by the Army who had left numerous knives, forks and spoons scattered and abandoned. These were quickly collected as they were hard to get and would prove useful when visiting hostels displaying the KFS sign in the handbook - which indicated that hostellers must bring their own. Even at this time the grounds of Alton Towers were beautiful with a profusion of rhododendrons, all in full flower. A later trip to St Briavels became memorable in the annals of Hinckley section, as it was here that Fred Bignall's socks caused trouble. He liked to hang them in the dormitory to air, much to everyone's discomfort, and when asked to remove them refused pointblank. When he found they had been put under his pillow sometime during the night, he was most affronted and hardly spoke for the remainder of the tour. Poor Fred never did see the point of the joke, although everyone else enjoyed it for years.

Winchester hostel was popular as there was a mill race through the cellar and brave souls could ride a wooden board suspended from a beam which dipped just below the surface of the water. The men's washroom was also down there and water was obtained by dipping a galvanised bucket into the racing water. Even more important, the hostel sold energy bars which were unobtainable elsewhere.

Duck eggs were easier to get than hen's eggs during this period of strict rationing and were often served at hostel breakfast. Packed lunches were two thick slices of bread, but the mainstay for food on tour were the British Restaurant canteens to be found in all large towns. Particularly good ones were remembered in Coventry, Oxford and Gloucester. A hot meal could be bought for 1/3d.

John remembers his first long ride was from Hinckley to Coventry where he saw the devastation caused by the bombing of the cathedral. The aftermath of the war is mostly remembered for the shortages of food, clothing and equipment. Everyone used something that had originated in the armed forces and ex-Army shops sprang up in every town. Rhona remembers a holiday she spent in Devon with Ruth Bennett and Ann France. They met some Americans wearing 'very unusual trousers' which they called denim jeans.

Ken Pepper, a rider with the Loughborough section, played a large part in encouraging John to take up cycle camping. Ken had bought a new tent and arranged to meet the Birmingham section at one of their favourite sites in the Towy valley. Unfortunately when John, Ken and Albert Sargeant arrived at Stratford on their first night's stop it was to find that only the flysheet was there, the tent having been left behind. Undeterred, they continued the tour and arrived at the Birmingham site in the dark at 9.30 pm.

They found a very orderly site with the latest camping gear in use. This was in contrast to their own old Army panniers, blankets with large safety pins and a groundsheet made out of old Army ponchos; all secured to their bicycles using rubber bands made from old inner tubes, with enamel mugs swinging from their bags. To their dismay, when they woke up the next morning, they found the Birmingham group up, packed and breakfasted. However, they did manage to meet up each night by following their route across fields and tracks. Revenge was sweet on the last day when, by chance, they met on the road home near Warwick. Thanks to the heavier bikes and gear of the Leicestershire trio and the fitness gained by pushing it all up hill and down dale, they were able to catch and pass the other group.

This tour proved a valuable lesson in what was needed for cycle camping. They bought new equipment and formed a camping section with John as the first secretary. Runs were organised every weekend. One joint Christmas holiday got off to a poor start when Ken confessed en route that he had been unable to book them into a hostel for the night So Christmas Eve was spent cycling until about 2 am when they found a convenient barn, with sufficient straw to keep everyone warm. Presents were exchanged early the following morning. Rhona remembers receiving a brooch from Betty (Naylor). After a quick wash in the stream, they carried on to their bed and breakfast - booked at Felindre where they again joined the Birmingham group.

DA and section events were important to the whole family and they took part in them all. One they remember was the 200 mile/24 hour in 1952, which for them began at Hinckley Grammar School at 4 pm on Saturday. They set off south with a strong wind behind them and made good time on their way to Worcester for breakfast. Further stops were made in Tewskesbury, Evesham and Warwick. But as they began the ride back to Leicester they realised the wind had gradually changed direction and was now blowing them back. This meant that they were in danger of arriving too early and being disqualified, so after a rest at Wolvey and an even longer (two hour) rest in Coalpit Lane, they were able to report to the marshal at Aylestone boathouse at 4 pm on Sunday.

In 1953, to celebrate the 75th anniversary of the formation of the CTC, it was arranged that a letter would be carried from the Mayor of Loughborough to the Mayor of Harrogate, by a group riding overnight. (It was in Harrogate that the meeting had taken place between Messrs Cotterell, Ineson and Cunningham on 5th August 1878, at which they formed a club known as the Bicycle Touring Club). It was a ride of approximately 100 miles for the Leicestershire group, with plenty of transport cafes open along the route for refreshment.

However, it was a very different story when John and Rhona repeated the ride in 1978, together with Ken Pepper, Jessie Hay and Tim Culpin. Ken was using the same map as 25 years before, but now the roads had changed. There were no longer transport cafes, as the traffic was using different roads. To add to their discomfort it was pouring with rain. Nevertheless the letter was again safely delivered to the Mayor of Harrogate from his counterpart in Loughborough.

Cycling days out were often helped by the use of the train, as cycles were not discouraged in those days. In fact a whole train was sometimes devoted to cyclists, who could be picked up en route. After a day's cycling everyone would rejoin the train for the return journey. It is easy to imagine the confusion that must have arisen as those getting off first tried to ensure their bicycle wasn't at the bottom of the pile in the guard's van.

On one of the usual Sunday runs the section was waiting in the Hollow at Earl Shilton when an elephant ambled by. Fortunately it was closely followed by the rest of the circus and so the run began on time. An essential piece of equipment for the run's leader was a piece of chalk. This was used to leave messages for late comers to help them catch up. Strict rules applied to these runs - never pass the leader, never get out of the saddle on a hill. If anyone did so, a cry would go up from the group "Saddle for sale." The speed was always that of the slowest rider, but they would still be covering approximately 100 miles a day during the summer.

Sandwiches were usually carried for lunch, but teas were booked and paid for in advance. Rhona and Anita recall the Fillongley cafe where tea and bread and butter cost 1/3d. With cake it was 1/6d and, when available, tinned fruit and evaporated milk brought the cost up to 2/6d. The slices of bread were always counted to prevent the fast eaters getting more than their fair share. Senior members had first choice of the cakes. This meant that the younger ones had only those that were left. Blakeshay Farm, near Newtown Linford, was a much loved venue for all local cyclists, especially in the winter on the shorter runs.

John recalls a very large rally at Fort Dunlop, at which everyone who attended was given a packet of patches, a valuable gift at that time as they were so difficult to get. Anita remembers having to carry one of the pennants, painted in DA colours and attached to a square section pole. She also remembers having to carry it back after the event as it was deemed wasteful to throw it away. It was a very colourful sight to see the pennants being carried around the arena followed by the riders from all the neighbouring DAs. Several thousand cyclists made an unforgettable sight.

During and after the war it was necessary to have a good memory for lanes, as there were no signposts and maps were hard to come by. If you were lost in Wales, life became almost impossible as the locals very often could not speak English.

By the end of this period Anita had met and married Terry Wykes and Rhona had met and married Bernard Brittain. Many of their friends had also married and started families. To provide more manageable family rides, Ed and Betty Broom started a family section, which included Janet and Sam Gabbitas and daughters; Eileen and Derek Blasdale and sons; Betty and Howard Naylor with Ann and Peter; plus Daisy and Ray Matthewman with Robin. Rhona, Bernard and son Paul were keen members of this new section. Rhona says that socials were very popular at that time, with the jelly made in an unused baby bath! The socials were often held at Quorn village hall, and it was not unknown for some people to stay there for the rest of the night, before cycling home the next day. Cricket matches in Bradgate Park were frequently organised between Hinckley and Charnwood sections and also against local YHA groups.

Bernard reminded us of the annual service held every May at Meriden. It was usual for the Hinckley section to obtain and take the DA wreath, as they had the shortest distance to carry it. This meant that someone had to carry it on their back, as no one attended in a car at that time. Each year the person who had carried it the year before was excused duty for that year, but would go back into the rota for the following year. On his first ride to Meriden, Bernard, who had just completed his National Service, found it impossible to get lost on the way there as every road was thronged with cyclists.

Fifty years later, many of the people mentioned here are still part of the Leicestershire DA cycling scene. Sadly Harold is now dead but he attended the Meriden service each year until his 90s. Rhona and Bernard are still very active in the Loiterers and Photographic section while John and Phyllis, although no longer active cyclists due to injury, are very supportive.

The wind reduced them to walking

Frank Forryan brought back memories of the time when he was DA secretary in 1950 and 51. He had joined the Loiterers section during the war and had ridden a tandem with his young daughter Mollie on the back on many YHA tours. In 1946 to Wales, 1947 to Yorkshire, 1948 to Minehead and the South West. These tours continued for some years.

He remembers that everyone wore shorts throughout the year, no matter how bad the weather. One night, round about 1947, the wind was so strong that it was lifting the roof of the stand at Grace Road up and down. On the same night Bill Duffin was injured when a chimney pot was blown into the road as they passed. Mollie remembers having to walk from Thurmaston to Leicester that night, as the wind was too strong for her to cycle against.

Frank also recalls a sad occasion when a motorist ran into the back of a group on one of the clubruns, killing one of the riders. On another occasion Phil Allen was caught without a front light on a late return and so was protected in the middle of the bunch of about 20 riders. Despite this they were spotted by a policeman and brought to a halt. On yet another occasion, Frank was stopped by the police and instructed to ride on the pavement.

He remembers that Bill Seagar had an elliptical chain set and they held concerts in a clubroom at the back of Bill and Connie Seagar's home - at one of these he remembers Janet Gabbitas being dressed up for the part. At one of the DA rallies, the John Bull factory in Evington Valley Road provided them with an inner tube to blow up to destruction. It took over 400 pumps before it exploded. "At least one of our AGMs was held in Leicester Town Hall at that time," he recalls.

Mollie married Owen Blower, who in 1958 was the RTTC British Best All Rounder. On his way to the championship Owen broke the 12-hour competition record covering 271.80 miles. Their two daughters Claire and Marie were both top class riders, the latter winning many championships. Claire was also a national coach.

An inner tube took 400 pumps before it burst

Howard joined - just for the handbook!

One of the DA's most loyal supporters over many years is Howard Naylor, owner of Beacon Cycles, Derby Road, Loughborough, husband of Betty who has also ridden with various sections since her teenage years.

Howard first joined the CTC in 1948, not to ride with a local section but to get a national handbook to help him find accommodation when on some of the long rides he undertook at that time. One of the first of these, at the age of 17, was a two day ride from Leicester to Norwich and then back. As he worked on the railways at this time, eventually becoming a fireman, Howard was able to obtain free travel. So he took himself and bicycle up to Edinburgh, allowing three days for his return to Leicester. These were to be three extremely wet days which meant riding against time all the way. First night at Carlisle, second at Long Preston finally arriving back in Leicester for the third night. He can still remember the taste of the apricot jam sandwiches which kept him going.

Following this, he was required to do his National Service for 18 months after which he was pleased to be released into the sort of job which allowed him to get back on to his bike. Still working for the railways, he got another free travel pass which took him up to Thurso, allowing 16 days of riding using both youth hostels and CTC accommodation on his way back home. During all this time, George Clowes who lived next door to Howard, had been a member of the loiterers section, so in 1951 Howard decided to join them on their Sunday run. This must have been in February, as they were all talking about the Valentine Dance they had been to the night before. The following Sunday he decided to ride with the photographic section - as they were two distinct sections then. He rode with both sections until about May or June when seven or eight of them got together and re-formed the general section. This was to allow longer rides for those who wanted to go further afield, eventually progressing to become the hardriders' section. One of their early rides was around the Wrekin and back (a reminder of the phrase "All around the Wrekin" when a description is long-winded).

All through the 1950s and beyond, all the different sections had regular socials on Saturday evenings and everyone travelled out to the various market towns and villages around Leicester to enjoy them. Howard clearly remembers helping to carry a baby bath full of jelly on the service bus from Leicester to Quorn, something which was not the slightest bit unusual.

A photograph from Alan Tyrell, featuring a group of various sections at a social in Quorn Village Hall in 1950

The first carol service was the brainchild of the general section and was masterminded by two members, Ray Pears, who lived at Stapleton and Pete Summers, who lived at Sutton Cheney. The tea rooms for this event were where the Woodlands Nursery now stands.

In 1953 Howard agreed to become the runs' secretary for the DA which involved organising the 12 and 24 hour standard rides and the 100 in 8 as well as the occasional roughstuff. He continued in this post for three or four years until Dave Gelder took over.

AGMs were held at 2 pm on Sundays in Regents Rd, Leicester. To make a day of it, they would get up early to ride to Warwick then back in time for the 2 pm start. New Year's Eve at Blakeshay Farm, down to the Bradgate for a drink and then up to Old John for the stroke of midnight.

On another occasion he recalls climbing to the summit of Ben Nevis wearing cycling shoes, going up wasn't too bad but it was a very long way back. On this holiday the route continued to Mallaig, but it was so hot the tar on the roads was melting and splashing up on to the frames.

They arrived just in time to see the ferry leaving on its way to Skye. This left them with plenty of time to clean their bikes as it was Saturday night and there was not another ferry until Monday! Howard recalls taking off the socks he had put on clean that morning and using them to get the tar off his frame!.

On one trip to Scotland, when the axle key broke in his Sturmey Archer gear, he was eaten alive by midges as he strugg led to repair it in the garage of a local pub. It lasted for the ride of 80-plus miles to Blair Gowrie the next day where he found a bike shop open - on a Sunday! There were yet more mechanical problems with a different Sturmey Archer which he repaired using cardboard and small paper pellets, distributed between the remaining ball bearings. This was good enough to last for a further two days.

During these years he met and married Betty. They had their children,

Pete and Anne, and continued their unbroken record of association with the Leicestershire DA through various sections. Loiterers, photographic, general, hardriders, family, Loughborough and now Charnwood. The move to Loughborough section was prompted by changing his job and moving to Shepshed, to live nearer to his new job in Derby.

He has always been a keen worker on behalf of his fellow members, has served on numerous DA committees and has been DA President. He is an active member of the Loughborough Road Safety committee and also served on the Leicester Accident Prevention Council when it used to meet at Charles Street police station. He has been a very generous supporter of our quarterly magazine Cycle Chat, providing financial help when it was struggling to survive. He is one of a long line of members over the ten decades who have made it possible for us to celebrate our centenary.

Breakaway group becomes backbone of the DA

An extract from an issue of the Loughborough Monitor of 1951 records that a Mr Phillip Allen went into their offices in 1950 to enquire about local cycling clubs. They were pleased to tell him that Mr KW Pepper, of the Cyclists' Touring Club, was the man to see. Many happy cycling miles later, with Loughborough section still growing, riders from the Ashby, Coalville and Whitwick areas decided they had enough keen riders to form a new section, to be known as Charnwood.

Many of these founder members are still supporters of the DA and participate in social events and occasional rides. Phil Allen, Frank and Nancy Holden, Adele Heafield, Stan Kent, Roy Johnson and Reg Fletcher are just some of the names remembered from that time. The inaugural run was to Repton Shrubs on the first Sunday in May 1951, with lunch at the Shakespeare. Phil described how he became a member of the CTC in 1950 by responding to an advertisement in Cycling and Bicycle while doing his National Service at RAF Benson.

He returned to Whitwick where he lived with his parents, got a job at Brush, Loughborough and joined a keen group of CTC members who rode with the Loughborough section. So began a lifelong involvement with the club. He recalls how Charnwood booked hot lunches in addition to tea and how favourite venues were visited on many occasions. At Blakeshay Farm near to Ulverscroft the teas were served at plain deal scrubbed tables, with benches for seats. Good farmhouse teas of boiled eggs, bread and butter and home made cakes would cost about

2/- with the chance of a game of football, cricket or rounders to follow. Plenty of tea, piping hot in large teapots, circulated making this very close to a cyclists' idea of heaven. Another local magnet was Annie's in Newtown Linford. She had tables and chairs on her small lawn but when it got dark, or was wet, she would welcome you into her tiny cottage sitting room where you sat on the floor when the chairs were full.

Hostelling was very popular in the 50s and 60s, with groups going away at Easter, Whitsun and the annual holiday break from work. In the first year (1951) the section went to South Wales and took the paddle steamer from Cardiff to Weston super Mare 'at CTC rates.' Somerset, Devon and Cornwall were all visited at different times and because it was so easy to take bicycles on trains, it was possible to return from Bath this way. Families often joined members of the club on these trips.

During the 60s and 70s, the section regularly enjoyed overnight rides to Harrogate and York, specially to visit the weekend rally held on York race course each year. In the early 1960s the DA rally was instituted at Blakeshay Farm and continued for many years at various sites around the area. Phil organised these rallies for a long time and local racing clubs and neighbouring DAs would enter the events in the hope of winning the coveted award. It was usually a fine day, but there was one year Phil remembers the rally being washed out. In later years the rally became the CTC's contribution to the calendar of the Leicestershire Cyclists' Association and was hotly contested by many clubs. Traditionally a tug of war was waged throughout the day, but when one year the Coalville Wheelers turned up with heavy boots and swept the board, it was decided to change the rules!

Phil has retained his interest in all things which involve cycling and now works very hard on behalf of Sustrans, the charity dedicated to providing safe cycling routes throughout Great Britain. He is also involved in cycle training for schoolchildren.

Two other founder members are Adele Heafield and Nancy Holden who both have fond memories of the early days of the section. Adele began her cycling days when a friend, Mary Jackson from Bradford, persuaded her to have a go. At that time they were serving in the WAAF, so Adele started off on a service bike, however the pedals kept falling off. Adele then asked her mother in Ashby to send her own bicycle up by train. During the journey someone stole the wheels and substituted a really old wrecked pair, with flat tyres, so before Adele could begin her new sport, Mary had to send to Bradford for some decent replacement wheels.

Adele's first ride was from Cheadle Hulme to Dovedale and return, a distance of 93 miles. Having survived this baptism of fire, she allowed her name to go forward as a prospective member. At that time your name was proposed by a member and displayed on the notice board for a month. Providing no one objected, you were allowed to pay your subs and become a full member.

One cycle tour Adele recalls was to Cornwall. This got off to a very poor start as it was raining heavily and blowing a gale when they left the train. There was nothing for it but to get on their bikes and make for the hostel at Otterham, down a narrow, spooky lane.

On another occasion Mary and Adele were setting off on holiday when an oncoming car blinded them and caused them to fall on to a pile of gravel by the roadside. Mary was so enraged by this she grabbed a handful and threw if after the car, to their surprise they heard it rattle on the boot, which so alarmed them they jumped on their bikes and pedalled away as fast as possible. (Is this the first recorded example of road rage?)

Frank and Nancy Holden were members of the Coalville Wheelers and regularly marshalled or rode their events. When Reg Fletcher asked if they would be interested in helping to form the new section, they were pleased to begin riding with it. Their daughter Jean, who was 10 years old at this time, enjoyed this different sort of cycling. Nancy remembers Scaddows Farm on the road between Ticknall and Hartshorne where you could have as many cups of tea as you wanted for 4d. The farm was next to one belonging to Ted Moult, a famous radio and television personality at this time. The tea was served in a large shed, a welcome sight to the many cyclists who used its facilities. A similar shed is at the Green Man pub, Clifton Campville and is still used by the section from time to time. Yet another favourite tea stop was the garden tearooms at Alrewas.

Some recollections from Nancy's long life in cycling are of baby daughter Jean grabbing at the roadside vegetation and almost bringing the tandem to a stop; wintry rides to the midweek clubroom at the Queens Head, Belton, when they always rode from Ashby despite the dark frosty conditions. Even fog did not prevent them going.

More recollections from Adele, Nancy and Brenda Randon seem to frequently involve water. Joe Upton, an early member of the section, liked to swim in any river on their route, although his favourites were Zouch and Barrow. Brenda took a more involuntary dip when she fell into the Trent and Mersey Canal, necessitating a return home in Alex Thomson's spare trousers and a top donated by Pearl Thompson. Alex was involved again when young Johnny Gadsby fell into the Manifold and Alex attempted to dry him out using the hand dryer in the men's toilets.

Adele led one run when a particular stretch from Thorpe to Bloor was a morass of mud. One member known as 'Appy Arry' never forgave her as he was out that day on a new bike and was quite disgusted at having to attempt to clean it in a nearby gateway.

One year, when the national BCTC came to Leicestershire DA, the catering was done at Oaks in Charnwood. Nancy, Bridget, Brenda and Anne were part of the catering team which produced such good food that Bill Catlow claimed it put professional caterers to shame.

Charnwood members have always enjoyed visiting the Birthday Rides, held at various venues up and down the country. One such occasion was to the Melrose Rides in 1980 when so many DA riders attended a coach was hired and the bikes travelled on a lorry provided by John Warne, a Loughborough section member.

Charnwood section riders have always been keen to support events and to provide officials to form DA committees. Many of their members have been DA secretary and have also been presidents and, in one case, national councillor. Today it is a section retaining the loyalty of long-standing members, as well as attracting new riders, just what's required for the start of the next 100 years.

A group from Hinckley on their way to the Carol Service in December 1967

DA President John Allen does things in threes with young Julie and Ian aboard

Enjoying the lazy, hazy days on summer in 1931

A group at Hoveringham in 1931

Tandems for two. Cyril and Lilian Jesson (at the back) with Florrie and Syd Wilson

Tube bursting competitions were always popular. Guess how many pumps to burst it and pay a penny. Winner takes all

The Hinckley group at Copt Oak on their way to Oaks in Charnwood

President's ride in Rutland during the eighties

Chance meeting began a long association

Twins Keith and Alan Lakin joined Charnwood Section in the summer of 1960. They had been to Darley Dale on their bicycles to visit friends when members of the section caught up with them at the top of Melbourne Hill. When it was discovered that Alan and Keith had ridden further than the others the pair were invited to join both the midweek run to Kings Mills and the following Sunday's run to Tutbury Castle - led by Frank and Nancy Holden.

They enjoyed themselves so much that they became members and continued to ride every week. Keith had an unbroken run of six years four weeks without missing a Sunday run. During that time both regularly took part in the competitive DA events, with intense rivalry as to who gained the most points. Alan was very good at map reading events but it was Keith who achieved the distinction of being the first Charnwood rider to qualify to ride in the BCTC final in 1964.

This was held in the south, starting from Godalming and finishing at Guildford. Keith finished a respectable 24th out of 40, a few places ahead of the late Ray Matthewman who had kindly given Keith a lift to the event. Although Keith continued to compete in the heats each year, he never again qualified for a place in the final. It was also in 1964 that the Leicestershire Best All-Rounder Competition resulted in a tie between Alan and Keith Lakin, although Keith went on to complete the hat trick by taking the BAR in 1965 and 1966.

Keith enjoyed touring and one memorable trip was led by Dick Thompson to Southern Ireland. Seven men and one lady went on the tour, using youth hostels along the way to the Ring of Kerry. The one lady, Pearl Blaza, was later to become Mrs Dick Thompson!

A lot of work was being done in the section for the cycle proficiency scheme at this time, with at least two evenings every week being devoted to training children at local schools. So successful was this venture that the section, led by Phil Allen, won the national Shell Trophy, awarded by the local Road Safety Committee. Keith very much enjoyed his involvement in this.

Sunday runs were varied, with swimming runs to the baths at Tamworth being very popular. There was also an annual run to Skegness. This always started from Grace Dieu Priory at 10pm on Friday and the riders reached Skegness in time for breakfast. After spending the morning by the sea, and having lunch, they would leave about 3pm to ride to Lincoln Youth Hostel for Saturday night before returning to Coalville on Sunday.

The standard of riding was usually very high, although Keith recalls one occasion when Phil Allen stopped the club run at Sutton on the Hill and left the riders in no doubt as to his opinion of their silly antics, before allowing them to continue.

The York Rally was always well attended with some members riding there while others hired a bus to make an outing of it with friends and relatives. The riders had to leave at about 3pm to be back in Coalville for midnight, while those on the bus left after the rally, often passing their colleagues somewhere near Bawtry.

Punctures and breakdowns were often remembered years later. Alan was still out at Beeston when he suffered an irreparable puncture. He had to stuff his tyre with grass to get home. On another Sunday, near to Monyash, the back wheel on Dick Thompson's tandem collapsed to the point where it couldn't be ridden. He borrowed Keith's bike to ride home to Markfield to collect his car. In the meantime Keith and

Pearl set out to walk to Ashbourne pushing the tandem. They were offered a lift in a Transit type van, which they gratefully accepted. They were dropped off in Ashbourne and continued walking towards Sudbury. It was at Great Cubley that Dick met them on his way back and they all piled into his car with the tandem on top. As a final twist to the day, they passed the rest of the section near to Burton on Trent as they were repairing a puncture.

Keith's interest in cycling waned during the 70s and early 80s due to family commitments, although he never completely lost touch with the section. He could always be relied on for help with marshalling and for supporting social events. In 1991 Keith and his wife Jean became joint secretaries of Charnwood section and so became even more involved in the day-to day running of the section and the DA. The couple continue to be involved in organising events, although they do not cycle regularly with the DA. Keith enjoys riding the roughstuff and freewheel events. Leila their daughter also likes to ride the freewheel. The family are part of the Birthday Rides '97 organising committee, with responsibility for the evening entertainment at Scraptoft College.

Route planning experts at Kibworth

Without the building of the Saffron Lane cycle track in Leicester at the end of the 1960s it's unlikely there would have been a Kibworth Section some ten years later. The track allowed the BCF to host the World Cycling Championships in 1970. Among those spectators visiting the county for the first time was Peter Witting, a regular rider with the South Bucks DA. He was attracted by the relatively cheap housing, quiet lanes and active cycling enthusiasts. So it was that Peter, his wife Barbara and their two children, Richard and Victoria, moved up-country.

By the mid-70s Peter had become secretary of the Leicester General section, as well as DA treasurer. With the growing community in Kibworth, and the absence of any DA section serving the south of the county, Peter raised the required number of signatories to form the Kibworth section - but using the sub-title Kibworth Cycling Club, to prevent the formation of any rival club!

Half-day rides were organised for youngsters, usually on a Saturday morning, leaving Sunday to join in DA events. A midweek clubnight was organised for socialising and learning route planning skills, and for trying to beat Anneka Rice on her TV Treasure Hunt. Tony Mellor was a professional at this activity, since he worked for the AA answering route enquiries.

Over the next few years it was rare that the DA map reading or BCTC trophy did not reside at Kibworth.

The section was responsible for introducing Audax events to Leicestershire. Nick Rosenthal had been riding 200km events with Peter from Telford. The DA committee agreed to replace the old 12 hour standard rides, over 130 or 150 miles, with the easier 200km distance. Subsequently the 100km Populaire distance was introduced, so everyone could enjoy Audax riding. Nick Rosenthal became the first DA member to complete the 1200km Paris-Brest-Paris Audax event in 1979, taking some 76 hours. Peter went on to complete the Centennial PBP in 1991.

Kibworth section members organised the full range of DA events, from BCTC heats, 100 mile and roughstuff standard rides, and the DA carol service. A number of newcomers to the CTC went on to play a part in the club's wider activities: Stephen Lee, a skilled route planner, helped Oxfordshire DA organise the Veterans' Triennial Rides some years later; while Angela Kirk became a CTC accredited tour leader, specialising in off-road and lightweight camping tours.

Fame of another kind was to embrace one-time Kibworth section treasurer Ian Hoxley, son of Leicester Mercury sportswriter Ken Hoxley. Whether influenced by the music heard at the section clubnight, or not, Ian's band became chart toppers! They topped the independent label charts, and were signed up by Virgin Records. Ian retains his CTC membership, as does his father, now editor of Cycle Chat.

By the late 80s the Kibworth section had not grown to a level to sustain its activities without the founders. Most of the youngsters had moved away to attend university. Peter Witting needed more time to ride events further afield, and Tony Mellor was planning his retirement bird watching in Norfolk. By now the Lutterworth section was fulfiling the needs of members in the south of the county, so it was an opportune time to wind up the Kibworth section.

Wife and children disappeared into an engine shed

William Moore, of Thorpe Satchville, offers an independent CTC member's viewpoint, although he supports the DA by subscribing to Cycle Chat.

My cycling started in the 1930s and I joined the club in 1935. My wife May and I, with our family, used to alternate the annual holidays in the Cotswolds and Wales, where we stayed at Aberystwyth. A favourite ride was up the Ystwyth Valley where we had a beautiful picnic spot by the river at Trwscoed and also near Strata Florida. I once took our son Andrew, when he was about ten, with a tandem, over the top and down the Towy Valley.

One amusing event was when we caught the train back to Aberystwyth from Strata Florida. I unloaded the bikes at the station then looked round for the family - they had disappeared! Eventually they turned up. It appeared that while I was not looking, all four of them had got on to the footplate and gone with the engine to the shed.

The railway staff were very kind and friendly in those days. It is a disappointment not to be confident in using the railways nowadays in conjunction with cycling. I have tried it, but found it too uncertain and have given up trying to take the bike on a train.

I did not ride with any section. I was engaged in other commitments in the 1930s, so my rides were usually solo. Most of my friends soon gave up cycling and, after the war, I married and my wife did not wish to ride in company.

We did ride tandem during a tour of Ireland in 1947. We had a second-hand Grubb with Trivelox gears. Later, when we had two children, we had an old Watsonian side car, then a kiddie seat at the rear. Still later, with three children, I saw the Taylor brothers at Earls Court Show and had a Jack Taylor triplet specially built and assembled by my cycle dealer, George Evans. His shop was in Humberstone Gate. Eventually all the children, as well as May, had hand built cycles. After George retired I went to Sid Mottram. My son who is now in Buckinghamshire, has my last bike supplied by Sid.

During the war I rode with members of the Hampshire Road Club, as I was in the Navy and on Hayling Island in 1941/2. Later I got some rides in Tunisia on duty activities. In 1944, when in India at Cochin, I enjoyed some rides in breaks from attending to moorings for landing craft. A special treat was a week's leave in the Nilghiri Hills with a hire bike, but the front forks broke and I landed on the dirt road with a bloody face and arms, but no serious injury.

In 1981 I did at last do some car-assisted riding in the Highlands and achieved my ambition of riding to Cape Wrath. Then in 1986 I rode in the Triennial Vets Ride centred at Market Bosworth, and have completed the 1989, 1992 and 1995 rides (the latter from Stamford).

On the 1992 ride I met an ex-Leicestershire man on tour from Canada. Hugh Hewes stayed one night with me as he was visiting some friends around Leicester. He came over last year and rode the event in Cheshire. I do not know whether he remembers any old members of Leicestershire DA or not. He now lives in Ontario. Some local CTC members may know him.

Family cycling at its very best

by Morgan Reynolds

Joy and Morgan Reynold's connection with the CTC in the Hinckley area began 30 odd years ago.

Joy and I moved to Earl Shilton in 1961 where our first daughter, Lynne, was born in the same year," says Morgan. At that time a section did not exist in the area - the golden days of the Harold Williams' family era had ended in 1956.

In 1962 we had Lynne awheel in a Watsonian sidecar used on a solo cycle. It was a super bit of kit, 12-inch wheel, boat shaped, silver oyster shell covering and a red leather hammock type seat. It was sluggish on hills and wanted to run away on the down!

Mandy came along in 1963, relegating Lynne to a seat behind Joy. We coped well with these, covering some reasonable Sunday mileages. However, in 1965, our third daughter Tracy was born, causing a major re-think. Two is easy, but three made us think hard. It was probably a year before we fitted Kiddycranks to our pre-war Hobbs of Barbican tandem, enabling Lynne to pedal. Young Tracy sat in front of me on the top tube and Mandy was seated behind Joy.

Anyway, it was late in 1966 when Ken Pepper, that CTC stalwart from Barrow-on-Soar, instigated a section revival for Hinckley. Eric Neal, Ernie Whitehead and David Bunting were also involved in the resurrection, and so it was in mid-December the first clubrun to the carol service at Cadeby took place.

Our first section ride was on the 19th March 1967, we are not sure of the destination, but it was probably Monks Kirby, just over the Warwickshire border. On 11th June of that year a group of us went to the Whitwick Rally, the first introduction for many of us to the Leicestershire DA. Phil Allen, from Charnwood, was a most competent organiser of the field events. That field at Whitwick was ideal, but alas the next year's event was to be the last one held there. Our daughters were then aged seven, five and three years and all awheel and we were honoured to win the Leicestershire Family Trophy.

The section settled into fortnightly Sunday club runs. Some of the riders we recall were Joyce and David Bunting, Janet and Eric Neal, Ernie Whitehead, with son John; and George Stephenson a lovely gentleman, originally from Liverpool. George told us stories of rides down the A5 to London as cyclists, collecting funds for the proposed Cyclists' Memorial on Meriden Green, eventually to be erected in 1920 after the First World War.

We had Kath and Dennis Heggs with Michael, Nigel and June - the boys being big enough to be strong solo riders. John Newberry and son Paul; Jimmy Moulds, the three-wheel enthusiast from Narborough; Gordon Ward and Keith Robey, from Nuneaton. Also young boys Robert Sweet, Jeff Morant and Robert Hampson, all of a tender age, joined us - much of the attraction being young Irene Wykes, the granddaughter of Harold Williams, our link, along with Eric, of the past section.

Our destinations were varied, with reasonable mileages and with the odd youth hostel trip included for good measure. We recall attending the 25th York Rally in 1969, another 'first' for many of us. I represented the section on the DA committee, meetings of which were held at Lansdowne Road School, just off the Aylestone Road in Leicester. Stalwarts I recall were David and Fay Gelder, Barry Broom, Geoff and Gwenda Fox, Ken Pepper, of course, Buster Haywood and Howard Naylor, with Ron Thorpe being an excellent chairman.

In 1970 I became involved with Bradgate Road Club, the racing off-shoot of the DA. John Newberry and I rode our first time trial , a 25-miler on the Six Hills. Another highlight in 1970 for us was winning the family (Raleigh Cup) trophy at the York Rally. Joy manned an old nameless tandem with Lynne as stoker. I was on our pre-war Hobbs of Barbican tandem, plus Rann trailer, with Mandy and Tracy on kiddy-cranks. We were beginning a week-long hostel tour of Yorkshire. Now we had the great big Raleigh Cup. What could we do with it? Luckily Trevor Page, our local cycle dealer, came to the rescue and transported it home. We must have been keen, for we won the cup again the following year -although we were much better organised by then!

Section runs continued apace, plus Wednesday evenings from April until September. These were popular, mainly with adults, with a 7 pm

The triumphant Reynolds family with the coveted family trophy at the York Rally

start from Rogues Lane, aptly named, on the corner of the A447 between Hinckley and Barwell. We would ride for about a couple of hours, then have a 'swift half' at a local hostelry before a short dash home. Several keen members continued the midweek rides throughout the winter. Quite often we would embarrass Police Sgt Dennis Heggs with our 'bobby-dodger' lights, but that is a story in itself!

We had several years of 'riding in the New Year'. This consisted of meeting around 9 pm, an hour or so ride to a country pub, then leaving on the homeward trail about half an hour before midnight. Finally we would gather around some lamp-post for Auld Lang Syne and then it was home to bed.

I was secretary at this time, taking over from Eric, I think. Anyway, some of our young, and not so young riders, fancied "having a go" in the local Hinckley CC 10 mile time trials, held on Tuesdays on the Wolvey to Cloudesley Bush course. These were a bit daunting for some, so for 1972 I formed our own Hinckley Velo, affiliated to the RTTC, and ran six summer monthly Wednesday evening trials on the course. They were fun. I recall the timepiece we used, a large photographic alarm clock with a huge sweep hand! It certainly impressed the real racing men. The Velo ran for two seasons before disappearing into history. Our stalwart, Eric Neal, rode at least one of the events, I think this should be recorded for posterity!

John Newberry took over the role of secretary in late 1972. We did not have too many officials. The section had always run in a simple way. My diary tells me that in 1974 all our three girls went 'solo' to Repton Shrubs, a trip of 62 miles, at ages 13, 11 and 9 years. And in 1976 we went to our first Birthday Rides, at Alnwick, Northumberland, with a good contingent from Leicestershire. They included Howard, Betty and Ann Naylor, John and Alan Hartshorne and Frank and Nancy Holden.

It was also in 1976 that the Bradgate Road Club opened its membership to other than CTC members. This followed the departure of Geoff and Gwenda Fox - who virtually ran the club. It was then that Joy and myself joined Hinckley CC.

In 1978 the CTC, celebrated 100 years, a fine century. As part of many celebrations, a relay ride from the top of the British Isles to the CTC headquarters took place in June. It was to enter Leicestershire at Croxton Kerrial and travel south across delightful country into Northamptonshire. I believe it was 7.30 am midweek when the Leicestershire contingent assembled at the hand-over point - Croxton, - to await the party from Notts and Derby. Joy and myself joined Eric and Janet representing Hinckley.

Elevenses were at the home of Mr and Mrs Philip Ennis where the subsequent group photograph showed Joe Upton, Peter Witting, Nick Rosenthal, Rhona and Bernard Brittain, Peter and Margaret Hopkins with son Colin, Phillip and family, Eric, Janet and ourselves.

Mid-afternoon saw the Hinckley quartet cycling home from the hand-over point - Corby, going via Foxton, where a pint of shandy went down a treat before reaching home with 101 miles under our belts. Later, on 5th August, the actual 100 years were celebrated in some style at Harrogate, birthplace of the CTC.

Gill and David Bull,with children Lynn, Jennie and Robert from Braunstone, were very prominent in the DA around this period. Known as the Taurus CC, they were organisers of some really excellent prize presentations as well as all sorts of challenging rides. Our girls went hostelling with them, and the weekends of the 'Skeggy' and back were a real challenge. Joy and I did the double trip on one particular Cup Final day - in order to be free on the Sunday!

By 1980 our girls were independent. With school exams, their cycling times were limited. In fact, Joy and I had our first solo week away in September that year, enjoying a fixed centre tour from a cottage in the Lake District. The girls remaining at home for the first time. Another era was dawning.

Keith Robey was the Hinckley section secretary by this time, putting fresh ideas into our activities. Our family direction was changing and we were less involved in the section activities and more with the DA, which was to lead into the successful 1984 Birthday Rides at Scraptoft. That's yet another chapter!

The 1978 Centenary Round Britain Ride. Leicestershire's contingent seen at the home of Phillip Ennis

Pedalling through five decades

by Peter Hopkins

I can date precisely the beginning of my love of cycling. My parents were not cyclists, but at Christmas 1949, when I was 14, they gave me my first new bike: a sturdy black Hercules roadster with oil-bath gearcase and (wonder of wonders) a three-speed hub. It replaced the small, decrepit secondhand Humber on which I had learned to ride during the War. So my real interest began just halfway through the Millennium.

By February 1950, my newly-fitted Lucas cyclometer told me that it was possible to pedal this solid dreadnought as much as 20 miles. Even 25 miles! Then 30 miles: I couldn't believe it! Each ride that spring I pushed myself a bit further until I topped 50.

I spent the first 19 years of my life on the Wirral, about two miles from the sea. For a cyclist, one of the snags of living on a peninsula is that you can set off in only one direction (that, by the way, is why I've lived inland ever since!) The first and last 15 miles of every run on the Wirral had to be the same. However, it did mean that cyclists were geographically concentrated, and this speeded my introduction to 'proper' cycling.

About 12 miles from my home there was a famous road junction known as Two Mills, where the Birkenhead- Queensferry (North Wales) road intersected with the West Kirby-Chester road. I knew nothing of 'real' cycling when I first came across this magic crossroads one Sunday in

March 1950. That morning a new world opened up for me: as far as my amazed eyes could see down the Chester and Queensferry roads there were bikes, bikes, bikes, propped four or five deep against railings and fences.

The Two Mills and Eureka cafes were packed to overflowing; everywhere groups of riders stood gossiping - and it was thus every Sunday, for here all the cyclists of Merseyside converged before heading into either North Wales or the Cheshire lanes. Thereafter, every Saturday evening I perused a column in the Liverpool Echo headed "Wheelers' Runs", listing the next day's destinations for at least two dozen clubs: Merseyside Wheelers, Liverpool Century, Liverpool Mercury, East Liverpool Wheelers, Phoenix CC Aintree, Birkenhead Victoria, Birkenhead North End, Wirral Olympic, Port Sunlight Wheelers - and so on, names I recall to this day.

From then on I was hooked. Looking closely at real club bikes, I soon realised that proper cyclists not only had dropped handlebars (which everybody knew anyway), but that they bound them incredibly thickly with layer upon layer of twill tape; even more strangely, they all rode single fixed wheels. And they had only one brake!

Although my only previous encounter with this simple transmission system had been on the front wheels of kiddies' 'Mickey Mouse' tricycles, it was the universally favoured gearing both pre-war and in the 40s and 50s for club runs (even hilly ones) and in all time trials from 10 miles to 24 hours. On these club runs everyone had capacious saddlebags; rear panniers were rare, bar bags very rare, and front panniers completely unknown; the exceptions were the derailleur-geared roadmen, especially in the BLRC, who favoured musettes or 'bonk bags', apparently made out of deck-chair canvas. (Whatever happened to bonk bags, by the way ? Tourists still used them at the Loughborough AIT Rally in 1972)

As for dress, older riders generally wore very baggy 'plus-fours,' but the less baggy 'plus-twos' were already coming in, and eventually became just 'plusses.' However, I did have a leaflet from Ossie Dover of Liverpool (well known as the Tricycling Tailor) which quoted for - and even sketched - some fantastically voluminous 'plus-sixes!' Man-made fibres were still in their infancy at this time; shorts were whip-cord or - for kids like me - khaki drill; capes were made of sticky oil-skin which produced a hideous ripping sound when you opened them!

Early in 1951, I traded in my Hercules Roadster for a Hercules Kestrel: £14 new, and actually boasting three plain gauge 531 frame tubes, but without any alloy fittings. With a group of teenage friends I founded the West Wirral Wheelers. My father started bringing home copies of Cycling for me (now Cycling Weekly); it cost 4d (about 1.5p). We learned quickly from Cycling. Racing heroes of the day included pro sprinters Reg Harris and Cyril Peacock and BBAR time triallists Ken Joy and Vic Gibbons; top lady was Eileen Sheridan. In road racing, then called "massed start," there was bitter rivalry between the conflicting codes of the NCU (National Cyclists' Union) and BLRC (British League of Racing Cyclists) - before they negotiated and then eventually amalgamated to form the BCF.

I still have a couple of copies of Cycling from those apprentice days. My special pride- and joy is their Diamond Jubilee edition of 25th January 1951. In it there is an article by BW Best (a former editor) in which he discussed the obvious truth that records cannot fall for ever. Modern riders will be interested in and, I think, amused by his comment on the '25' record: "I see the 25-mile figures (now at 58 minutes by George Fell) expressed with a '55' before finality's curtain drops." How wrong even an expert can be!

At Easter 1951 I went with a friend on my first short YHA tour: Ilam Hall, Edale and Oakenclough. Until that trip I had never heard of the Peak District, as North Wales was our 'natural' touring area. I'm pleased that my first-ever hostel is still open 45 years later, but a 15-year-old today couldn't join the YHA for two shillings (10p) as we did, or spend a night at Ilam (evening meal, bed and breakfast) for one shilling and eight pence (8p). The bed, incredibly, was four old pence for under 16s and nowadays that night at Ilam would cost a 16-year-old £13. 10 - nearly 73 times as much! I cannot remember whether we had to produce our ration books on those trips, and we certainly had to take our own knife, fork and spoon. Needless to say, there were so many cyclists and walkers that hostels admitted only 'own steam' travellers - and motor travel was explicitly ruled out until well into the 1960s.

Of course, I didn't realise it at the time, but I took to the road when cycling was on the crest of a wave. In those early post-war years very few people could afford cars - and even for the wealthy there were waiting lists and petrol rationing (happy days!) Most main roads were quiet, but there were hordes of cyclists out on Sundays, with tandem-and-sidecar a particularly common choice for family transport. CTC membership rose rapidly in the late 1940s to peak at 53,000-plus in 1950, and this was the biggest since the all-time record of 60,000-plus in the booming 1898-1900 period 50 years earlier. As I became more experienced during the Fifties, during National Service and at university, I became a more adventurous tourist and did a little utterly undistinguished racing. By now, I had my first 'real' custom-built bike - a Stan Butler made by Allins of Croydon, bought with some Army back-pay.

Alas, the Swinging Sixties saw a steady and remorseless decline in cycling; CTC membership fell to something like 18,000 before the end of the decade. About 1959, Prime Minister Harold Macmillan had made his famous pronouncement "Let's face it, most of our people have never had it so good." Increased prosperity meant that many people who had never expected to own a car in their lives now found it possible. A cynical Bradford cycle dealer observed to me in 1968 that the great post-war cycling boom - then so nostalgically recalled - really had nothing to do with love of cycling, but had been born of necessity: people simply couldn't afford anything "better". As soon as they were able to buy a family car, he said, the bikes rusted in the shed. I fear there was some truth in this, and only the dedicated cyclists remained (the elder statesmen and women of the DAs now!) Even these devotees often owned a car as well - and, I confess it, that did include me.

But we did at least keep the pedals turning. The DAs continued organising their programmes, the clubs their races. Throughout the Sixties, now resident in Leicestershire, I took party after party of boys YH touring in school holidays and on weekends during term. (One of these lads was a 12-year-old on a flat-barred, Sturmey-geared roadster; his name was Ken Platts. On Ken's tours, my co-leader was a youngish policeman and parent named Dennis Heggs, whose son Michael was in the party.) I felt that, even if these young tourists didn't remain cyclists for life, as Ken has, at least they would have had a worthwhile experience, and - equally important - seen roads and traffic from the cyclist's saddle when they later became voters and lawyers, motorists and town-planners.

In 1968 I was a founder-member of ESCA, the English Schools Cycling Association, which promoted all forms of racing in several age-categories, and encouraged touring with an awards scheme and inter-school competitions and trophies for YH bednights. This period, the early 70s, produced Leicestershire riders such as Chris Wreghitt, later to become National Open Cyclo-Cross Champion and Bianchi professional, and John Richardson, nowadays very active as an officer of the Loughborough Cycle Users' Campaign. Most of these lads enjoyed 'mixing' it: Chris achieved an ESCA Gold touring award and took part in a BCTC Final; John raced regularly and was in the winning team of the Leicestershire. GHS '10' heat.

In 1971 the Tandem Club was founded. Before then, when out on the tandem, Margaret and I frequently encountered nostalgic 'Oldies' who would say reminiscently "Ee, I haven't seen one of them for years!" - while children, who had never seen or even heard of such a beast, would call out in amazement "Look at that Double Bike!" So rare were they that we were becoming desperate for spares for our USWB Claud Butler, and we immediately joined the new club in the hope that there was a future for tandems. There certainly was !

I mention the Tandem Club and ESCA because their successful growth during the 1970s coincided with - and probably reflected - a cycling revival in that period, for the decline in CTC membership was reversed. No one could now argue that the increased numbers were cyclists through economic necessity. Many were 'come-back' riders in early middle age: the delights of the car had palled, happy club days were recalled, and expanding paunches viewed with rueful concern. Others had, at last, picked up the 'health' message and saw the virtue of taking exercise in an increasingly sedentary society. And other high-principled souls were sincerely concerned about the environment, about the use and depletion of fossil fuels, about the spread of tarmac and concrete, about escalating traffic snarl-ups, and about the stink.

We have some particularly happy CTC memories of the 1970s. This decade saw the beginning of the Birthday Rides (we recall Ipswich, Alnwick, Salisbury, Harrogate, Ludlow, Melrose, with affection) and we were very proud when Loughborough hosted the 1972 AIT Rally, superbly organised by Ken Pepper. Then came that memorable centenary year, 1978, with so many events: relay ride round Britain, Leicestershire camp and rally, overnight ride to Harrogate, souvenir plates, badges, ties, invitation rides . . .

Through the 70s and 80s I have seen this resurgence bring welcome spin-offs. "Double bikes" are by no means rare now: you can even buy them off the peg. The range of equipment and accessories - cycle bags, for instance - has expanded to offer a bewildering choice. Town-planners are being made to take cycling seriously. The government is said to want to encourage people to get out of their cars and walk or cycle, especially for those local journeys and the short trip to work.

There has, of course, been one other major development - an American import which brings us into the Nineties. On my last school YH tour in 1989, every single boy had a typical mass- produced sports bike with dropped handlebars ('racers' they would have called them.) Only Margaret and I were riding mountain bikes, then new, as a test-run for a cycle-camping tour in France later that year. I now know that if I had led any tour from about 1991 onwards, then not a single boy would have had a dropped-handlebar bike; every one of them would have had a mountain bike. Few kids want anything else, though it has much more to do with fashion than any urge to do Rough Stuff. The only reservation I have about mountain bikes is that a new, separate cycling culture seems to have sprung up with them - and one which has no link with the traditional cycling community. This has never happened before when something new has appeared, such as cyclo-cross, to say nothing of the fact that 'different' machines (such as tandems, trikes, Moultons) have always been part of the club world. I hope assimilation will come; cycling will be the better for it.

Except for three years, my life since 1960 has been spent in Leicestershire. On the minus side, that period has seen the spread of the car, and its consequences: the arrival of the M1, the M69, the M42; the development of the East Midlands Airport and Donington Racing Circuit where there had been some lovely quiet lanes; the 'discovery' of the Old Fosse by motorists; the appearance of Sunday markets and huge car boot sales - and so on. But, on the plus side, the CTC has always had a wonderful DA here: alert in safeguarding our interests, active in the promotion of a wide range of events throughout the year, and - above all - welcoming. Given this, I see no reason why the next century should not be just as successful as the one we are now proudly celebrating.

Newspaper boys and girls helped swell section numbers

Loughborough section was the first to be formed from the DA in 1922 and continued for at least six years until 1928. Diaries, borrowed from Stan Bray, indicate that another Loughborough section was formed in 1939 from the ashes of the Loughborough Wheelers. Records also show that a Shepshed section was formed in 1952 and was merged with Loughborough a year later.

We know from the formation of the Charnwood section that there was a large membership in Loughborough at that time. Ken Pepper is a name that re-appears again and again in the history of the DA. Unfortunately he felt unable to contribute his memories due to other pressures, although he was a tireless worker during the times he was active in CTC affairs.

The tale is taken up in 1975 when John Williams (formerly Hinckley and camping sections) with Phyllis and Gareth moved to Shepshed to take over the post office and newsagents. At that time Peter, Margaret and Colin Hopkins, Jessie and Ian Hay and Les Kirk were the few riders representing Loughborough. Due to his connections with Leicestershire DA John knew that Howard and Betty Naylor were still active and so contacted them for information on the local cycling scene. They put him in touch with Peter and Margaret Hopkins, who welcomed the Williams family into their group. There were no formal runs lists other than DA events. Everyone contacted the others to arrange cycle outings. However, they were all very enthusiastic about riding as a group which proved a magnet to other cyclists in the area. John Williams helped this along by encouraging his newsboys and girls, to come out on the runs, after they had delivered the papers. This also extended to their families, who swelled the ranks of the section. A major reason for the success of this new section was undoubtedly the PR work done by Peter Hopkins, who wrote each week for the Loughborough Echo. He managed to include the names of all the newcomers, as well as paying tribute to those who were by now old hands.

The big success of this section is the annual mince pie run, which began in 1978 when Ian and Jessie Hay invited eight riders to their home in Long Whatton on the Sunday before Christmas - for a cup of tea and mincepie. They were Peter, Margaret and Colin Hopkins, John, Phyllis and Gareth Williams, Mike and Tim Culpin. In 1979 the section had decided to invite other people to their run and considered hiring a hall. Some members were very dubious about this, so John and Phyllis agreed to guarantee the price of the hall as their contribution.

Peter worked very hard to publicise the Long Whatton Village Hall event on Radio Leicester, Nottingham and Derby, as well as sending invitations to all the local racing clubs. Of course the other Leicestershire sections were already well aware of the plans. Tea, coffee and mincepies, made by wives, sisters, mothers and girl friends were served to well over a 100 cyclists.

In 1980 a move was made to Belton Village Hall which offered larger facilities and Jessie took on the job of catering co-ordinator for the team which was to provide refreshments for the next 12 years. This team consisted of Margaret and Peter Hopkins, Phyllis and John Williams, Mike and Rhoda Culpin, Howard, Betty and Anne Naylor.

In 1980 nearly 300 hungry cyclists arrived for their refreshments but in 1981 numbers were drastically reduced by heavy snow, although even under these conditions over 80 riders overcame the elements to sample their mince pies. By 1982 the numbers attending the mince pie run had jumped back up into the hundreds and over subsequent years only minor variations in numbers have been experienced. More than 500 attended on one occasion, although actual numbers have not been recorded since those early years.

Some of the eigthy riders returning from the mince pie run in 1981

Jessie Hay, the stalwart of so much in the section, retired in the early 1990s and was presented with a carriage clock subscribed to by members and friends of the section. It was not long after this that Jessie became very ill and died, mourned by all who had known her.

The mince pie run is now a must on the calendar of cyclists from all surrounding areas and provides an excellent venue to meet friends on the Sunday immediately before Christmas each year. New faces are on the team, who have to work extremely hard to provide all the refreshments, but they are still recruited from Loughborough section members, led by Fiona Roche and Pam Cottle.

By 1981 the number of active cyclists in the section had risen to 124 as shown by the Beacon Trophy result sheet. Joint winners of this trophy were Ken Pepper and Trevor Staples each with 170 points. First junior lady was Jane Milligan with 157 points, Senior lady, Anne Naylor with 152 points. John Newport received a tankard as first boy novice and first girl novice was Alison Hough. The family trophy was taken by John, David and Andrew Marshall.

Members of Loughborough section were concerned that young riders were being lost to the CTC once they became interested in racing. This would not have mattered if they continued to ride with their new clubs. However, many of them joined a racing club, and because they were not able to match the times of established riders, they became discouraged and stopped cycling. The idea of forming a racing club, closely associated with the CTC took shape and a meeting was called for the 4th November 1981 at which it was agreed that the Loughborough Phoenix CC be formed.

There was some opposition to this move, as it was felt that the new club would draw members away from section activities. This proved to be unfounded - quite the reverse in fact. Young members came to ride evening events and went on to join the section on their Sunday runs. Only CTC members can become full members of Loughborough Phoenix. Open events are not allowed to be run on Sundays. The exception to this rule was in Cyclo Cross. This took place at Roecliffe Manor on a Sunday late in January each year. It was very well supported and provided much needed income for the Cheshire Home, as everyone paid a small admission charge to the grounds, which went to the Home. Chris Wreghitt Britain's top international cyclo-cross rider and national open champion for a fourth successive year agreed to become President of this new club.

Chris had been a pupil in the school in Loughborough at which Peter Hopkins taught and had ridden for some years with Loughborough section, taking part in local touring competitions. The Phoenix existed primarily to provide racing facilities for CTC members and also to train young novice riders to take part in other aspects of cycling.

This year (1997) is the 16th year of Loughborough Phoenix, but sadly a lot of the close co-operation between it and the section has been lost, although some of the riders are still active in both groups. A very social atmosphere is obtained on Wednesday evenings throughout the summer when the evening events take place on the West Leake circuit. Tea is made by the roadside and everyone is welcome, especially families supporting their own riders.

The problem all sections face sooner or later is that of riders becoming fit and enjoying long fast rides. This puts off people attracted to either half day rides or shorter runs at a gentle pace. To overcome this difficulty Trevor Staples suggested that a sub-section be formed to meet every other Sunday, to cater for these riders. Again there has been success - not only did it attract back members who had stopped riding with the section, but riders who were not yet members of CTC decided to join. Indeed the DA secretary, Ray Clay, became a member in this way.

Hostel weekends are a frequent feature of Loughborough section activities and many members take cycling trips abroad. The photographic competition has been run by them over the last three or four years in conjunction with the annual Slide Show. This is held in November at St Andrews Church Hall, Leicester Forest East. Each year a cyclist is invited to present slides of their holidays. In 1996 it was Trafalgar Square to Cape Trafalgar (Spain) by Ian Hill of Derby DA - a record of his ride over this fixed Audax route. Previous years have included Poland, New Zealand, Papua New Guinea, China and Round the World with our DA. The section also have occasional winter slide shows at John Storer House .

Yet another recent venture by local members Ariadne Tampion and John Catt, is the family section, formed after the birth of their daughter, designed to provide suitable distances and venues for young families.

Oh for the nights that are spent in camp!

by Alan Hartshorne

Cycle camping can be great fun. You either love it or hate it. I find it enjoyable and quite relaxing, especially on my own. You are independent - not that you can camp anywhere. One time I was camping near Kyle of Lochalsh and was head butted by a hedgehog ! It really happened, honestly. The hedgehog ran head first under the flysheet and made contact with my head through the inner. He visited me again the next night, but not so violently.

On the Isle of Skye I was visited by a wild cat, and at Applecross I woke to the crash of antlers as stags fought on the campsite for superiority. So you see camping can bring you very near to nature. Another year I camped in the Forest by Loch Rannoch. There was a wonderful sunset and next morning I emerged from the tent to find there had been a frost. With the sun shining through the fog on the frost, it made all the grass and trees glitter. It was magic! It was only 1st September!

Occasionally it rains, although to hear the Loughborough section, it always rains on my holidays. But after a day's cycling in the rain I find it really nice to sit in the tent, warm and watching the rain coming down.

Twice I have found myself camped in really windy conditions. Once, just north of Ullapool on a wonderful evening, I camped behind a bank but the wind got up and you could hear it passing through the telephone wires above. Then it seemed to bounce off the hills and come back from two different directions. I really found just how flexible my tent pole was! The other time was in Wales with my brother John. We camped on top of a cliff and it blew strongly at night for days. All the frame tents around us were collapsing. This campsite had a little valley which the sea swept into one night and carried away a large inflatable.

I now use Epigas to cook with. Their stoves are quite good. I did try petrol, but after a accident on the Isle of Skye, when a sheet of flame shot down the hill with me chasing after it trying to put it out, and another time when the stove exploded in flames, I gave it up. So if anyone wants a petrol stove....!

Camping with groups, such as at the Birthday Rides, Meriden weekend and, of course, York, is great, especially on the lightweight site. But it does have certain disadvantages. This year it was George's snoring - it made the ground shake. But also coming from another tent "Graham, did you do have to do that in here?"

Some years ago in the peak district this conversation was overheard in the middle of the night:

"David what are you doing ?
" I'm looking for my hat.
"What are you looking for your hat for ?
"My feet are cold !"

But I have found cycle camping as a group or on your own can bring a lot of enjoyment, and I have met a lot of nice people through it, which is surely what life is all about!

The tour leader

by Eric Neal

Basically, my qualifications for being a CTC tour leader came to the fore some 30 years ago - 1967 to be more precise, although the full potential wasn't realised until some years later.

One has to get the confidence of other people and this can come in many ways. Mine started with a small group of cycling friends, some of whom are still around today. Janet Cooper, warden at Copt Oak Youth hostel from 1974 to 1984, was one of my earlier 'recruits.' I had contact with her in the planning of the BCTC (British Cycle Touring Competition) final, which was held in the Loughborough area.

In her youth Janet had ridden a bike, but had stopped when her young family came along. Confidence on the road had gone. She was keen to have another go, but she hadn't got a bike that was suitable, a lightweight. So that was the first problem to be overcome. We visited Beacon Cycles in Loughborough, run by another close friend, Howard Naylor, and found a suitable machine. But how were we going to get it back to the hostel? It is all uphill from Loughborough!

It was a real struggle at first, but she made it and in time she became fully confident and began to venture further afield. She has been on many of my tours since and talks to her friends about Eric Neal's sunshine tours - it seldom rains when she comes along.

Another of my team, until his death in September 1995 at the age of 87, was Greville Marples from Poole, Dorset. He would never hear a word said against me and was a character who will be very difficult to follow. On some of his earlier tours with me he would carry two small transistor radios, one for the 'shipping' forecast at one o' clock and the other to listen to the music on Radio Four.

We were on a tour of Southern Ireland one time and it was about two minutes to the one o' clock forecast. It was raining heavily, the wind was almost gale-force, and here was 'Grev' (as he was better known to his friends) standing behind a rock for shelter in the Gap of Dunloe, waiting to hear about the weather. "You know what the weather is doing, it's p.........down," I told him. And so it was, but that was 'Grev.'

Then there are the 'whingers' in the party. Yes, we do have them, unfortunately. There is a case in point on a youth hostel tour. I was informed that I was making a profit of 50p per person. Was I aware of this? I did my best to justify the excess amount - but he didn't come again.

On a trip to the States, one lady insisted on single accommodation. I complied with her request in the main, yet didn't get a "thank you" when it was all over. Fortunately this type of individual seldom comes along again.

Most leaders are naturals, they have a flair for the job. There are exceptions of course and I've met some of them. In fact I joined some of them on tour - but I wouldn't do so again. What is not realised by some people is that, when you see a tour advertised, work has already been going on for months previously. Roughly speaking, it takes about 18 months to plan an overseas tour. Then there is always the late enquirer - we try to do our best!

At national level the club imposes certain conditions on tour leaders, but these are flexible and most of the time leaders are given a free hand with support, if necessary.

I have enjoyed leading tours and meeting people for the first time, they are usually the easiest to deal with. Familiarity tends to creep in with the folks who come again and again - I suppose it takes all sorts to make a balanced party.

Countries I have visited over the years include: Japan, Indonesia (Java and Bali), the United States, Poland, the Czech Republic, Slovakia, Morocco, Equador, Vietnam, Mexico, Norway, Sweden, Denmark, France, Germany, Spain, Portugal, Ireland and the Netherlands.

And I've always used the same bike, a Mercian. My saddle dates back to 1953, can anyone beat that? At 65, do I intend calling it a day? Definitely not!

Audax - made for the mile-eaters

There is an organisation catering for the needs of long distance cyclists which has been in existence for almost as long as the CTC. This is Les Randonneurs Mondiaux, the world wide body of Audax riders. A member of this organisation is the Audax Club Parisienne (ACP) which organises the Paris - Brest - Paris Audax every fourth year. This is a 1200km event, held in late August, for which it is necessary to qualify. Only Super Randonneur riders who have ridden and qualified in 200, 300, 400 and 600 km events in the same year as the PBP are entitled to ride. Furthermore, it is important to do the 600km early in the year, as applications have to be made by June. The entry fee for the last PBP was £50.

An Audax event is "a pre-determined, controlled route over distances of 200km and above at speeds of between 9 - 18 mph. Populaire events are those for distances below 200km."

British riders wanting to ride the PBP had to travel some quite long distances to qualify, which made it very difficult. In the early 1970s John Nicholas, with others, decided to form a branch of the ACP in Britain to enable our riders to qualify. Now Audax UK, with ACP, are fellow members of Les Randonneurs Mondiaux. Even so, it has been estimated that the cost of going to all the qualifying events, doing the recommended mileage of 200 miles per week, plus the cost of travelling to France, with accommodation, can be as much as £1500. This may explain why the average age of participants is 47.

Leicestershire rider Nick Rosenthal rode the PBP event in 1979 by being 'economical with the truth' on his entry form. His time of 73 hours 14 minutes made him the youngest rider, at 17, to finish the course. This does not appear in the official results, as the minimum age for entrants is 18. Nick had been riding long distance events since he was 14 when, following a touring trip through France, he rode the New Mills to Kegworth and back in the autumn of 1976. Following this, he rode the Windsor to Chester and then in 1978 the Centenary event from Cambridge to Aberdeen. This was 500 miles, which he completed in 42 hours, riding through two consecutive nights for the first time, experiencing hallucinations during the second night.

By this time he had made friends with a very experienced long mileage rider, John Chadwick, who told Nick of an experience he had while riding the Paris to Harrogate event in 1978. During the second night he was riding through the Fens and was absolutely convinced that he had seen a steam train falling from a viaduct! John Chadwick is now in his 80s and confessed in his 1996 Christmas card to Nick that he is no longer a mile-eater and can only do 100 miles a day in the summer- when it is warm.

Leicestershire DA has some keen Audax riders and Peter Witting organised our first 200km AUK event in the early 70s. This replaced the old DA standard ride of 130/150miles in 12 hours. Peter was one of the Leicestershire DA members who rode the PBP in 1991, which was also the Centenary of the formation of the Randonneurs' club. Peter took 83 hours to do the 1200km (750miles) Vince Bicknell, from Lutterworth, and Stephen Ralphs, Loughborough, were two other Leicestershire riders in that Centennial event. Stephen had first entered the event in 1987, but had been unfortunate to fall off after 40 miles in very wet and greasy conditions. He hurt his knee but got back on to his bike and managed another 200 miles before he was forced to retire. Later he found that the fall had also damaged his bike, when it was pointed out that he was leaving two trails on the road after riding through a puddle. Sid Standard, of Beeston, found that not only was the frame out of track but the front forks were damaged and the crank bent.

Stephen had had one successful ride in 1987 when he did Land's End to John O'Groats within the time to achieve the Gold standard. The previous occasion he took part was in 1983 when he managed the Silver standard. (Gold is for 1400km within approx 80hrs - Silver within approx 108 hours). During his 1987 ride, Stephen also suffered from hallucinations. He started at 2pm on a Sunday afternoon from Land's End and rode throughout the night and all next day, intending to arrive at his booked bed and breakfast at about 11pm.

However, he fell behind his schedule and began to struggle as he climbed over Shap. He found that quite ordinary objects appeared to be something else, a pile of stones could look like a child, or a tree like a house or a person. When he reached the top and began the descent to Penrith, he was actually falling asleep on his bike. He now admits that he was lucky not to go over the edge on some of the bends. Stephen finally reached Penrith at 1 am, two hours down on his schedule. He then failed to hear his alarm clock at 4am, eventually awoke at 7.30am believing that he had 'blown it.' But as he started on the route, it was to find that the wind had changed and was strongly behind him all the way to Edinburgh. At this point he was back on schedule and riding well. This didn't last, and although it was July, the last 200km was in the cold and wet, with the wind against him. But he still made it well inside the 'Gold' time.

In 1989 Stephen successfully rode the 1300km London - Edinburgh - London, but because the only other event he had done that year was a 600km he was not even a super randonneur. Due to illness, he was unable to ride this event in 1993, but hopes to complete it again in this our centennial year 1997.

By 1991 he again qualified for the PBP. He seemed to be going very well at Brest, but it was extremely hard on the return, with a freshening head wind all the way. His final time was just under 69 hours. By the time the event came round again, in 1995, he was having some trouble with his back but managed to get all the qualifying events in time. He started from Paris with sciatica and was disappointed at Brest to find he was six hours down on his 1991 time. But from here things looked up. His back pain disappeared and he 'flew' to the finish in a total time of 64hrs 35mins. He was sixth overall in the 1995 Audax championships. During 1996 Stephen rode five 200, two 300, three 400 and one 600km.

Ron and Eileen Johnson took a short break in Boulogne to ride the 'En Haut Pays D'Artois' on 20th September 1992. Eileen thought this would be easy, as they were on the tandem, and everyone knows that the terrain is flat on the other side of the channel! She found that this was a terrible mistake as she struggled up the hill from the ferry to the hotel. The next day was spent riding around the area hoping that the ferocious hills were not going to be on the Audax route. They were! Nevertheless, it was a super weekend and they finished in the qualifying time.

Dennis Heggs has also ridden in one of the French Audax events. His was 'Le Trois Vallees' also known to British Audax riders as the Dieppe Raid. Trophies play a very prominent part in French cycle events and Audax is no exception. They are presented immediately after the event and the recipient keeps them. They are not annual awards. On this occasion Dennis was presented with the Audax UK trophy. He is dedicated to riding Audax and enjoys visiting other areas throughout the year. He has organised the Leicestershire DA event since 1990 and is noted for providing good weather.

He was recently described by Keith Mulligan as Mr "I'll provide the weather'" Heggs, and hopes that the change from June to August (for the 1997 Birthday Rides) will not upset his reputation. The long ride which Dennis most enjoys is not strictly speaking an Audax. It is the 'Wild Wales' held over the late August Bank Holiday weekend. He has ridden this for the last 11 years, together with Don Jones of Rugby and Bill Hayward of Nuneaton. It starts and finishes at Bala with a slightly different route each year. However, most years include the Bwlch-y-Groes, which is notorious as being the highest, longest, steepest path in Wales. But the event is not considered to be 'wild' enough without it. Despite these feats of endurance by the hard men it is Dennis who has become Leicestershire DA's "Mr Audax."

Vince Bicknell, who was a member of the Lutterworth section, rode many Audax events around the country while qualifying to ride the Centenary PBP in the same year as Peter Witting and Stephen Ralphs - 1991. He completed this gruelling ride in 79 hours. He too has ridden the London - Edinburgh - London event starting at Doncaster and going north to Edinburgh, then all the way down to London before turning back towards Doncaster and the finish. This ride was 1300kms. No time is given as it is not usual to publish finishing times for AUK events. Suffice to say Vince was within the stipulated time.

Not everyone takes riding Audax events seriously. They are always worth riding as they cover some of the most beautiful scenic routes, and the time challenge adds just a little spice to a day's ride with friends. In 1986 Ron Johnson and John Allen decided to ride the South Pennine RC 200km Audax, which took them from Etwall up to Matlock, through Chatsworth into Grindleford. On to Ladybower and over the Cat and Fiddle to Glossop, Chapel-en le-Frith with the return route via Buxton, Ashbourne, Uttoxeter, Needwood Forest and back to Etwall.

Eileen and Ivy supported them by crossing the route at various points, offering drinks and refreshments. On one of these occasions Eileen asked them if they would like a sponge handing up, but John preferred to stop further down the road for it. Imagine the look on his face when he was given a soft squishy thing full of holes and water when he had been looking for a slice of Ivy's sponge, full of cream.

Finally, a story which perhaps epitomises the spirit of Audax riding. In 1983 Jeff Morant, of Hinckley, was set on riding the PBP event and qualified by riding all the necessary distance events. However, in doing so he ran out of cash and could not find the money necessary to go to Paris for the ultimate test. But like many cyclists, Jeff had a very understanding wife and she agreed they should sell a three-piece suite which they had bought only a year earlier. It raised £400 and Jeff was able to go to Paris after all. He completed the ride in 83 hours!

The trials of a Randonneur bike

by Dennis Heggs

Reprinted from Cycle Chat July 1994

I thought he was up to something when he fetched me out of my nice, dry winter quarters. It was in October he had dragged me around those Derbyshire hills and, while the effort had made me creak, it was nothing to the noises coming from him, especially that bit when he was climbing up Wynatts Pass. After that, he cleaned me up, even put polish on, fed my bearings and put me away for a nice winter's rest - no doubt even forgot me!

My shed mate, a small wheeled hussy, used to lean against me in all her mud and dirt and complain of where he had taken her, among the mud and water; so much so that, at times, she had given him a scare by twitching her back wheel in the mud. Serve him right, I say.

It was in February that I began to feel nervous as I noticed him beginning to look at me and especially when he used to pat and stroke my saddle! And then it happened - he wheeled me out and hoisted me aloft and started tinkering around with me. Before you could say "Randonneur," I found myself heading north again. But he treated me kindly this time and tried to avoid the hills.

I was put in a shed at that nice Youth Hostel and I had a lovely night chin wagging with those soul mates I recognised from last year's trials. By the way he rode me home, I realised my rest period was over.

Yesterday I was hauled aloft again and he went through his usual manoeuvres. He even bought me a present and fitted some nice, new jockey pulleys on my gears and taped over the gaps in my handlebar tape. I did feel posh!

In the morning, it was still dark as he put me in the back of his car and gave me a ride. When he unloaded me I soon recognised my mates of last year. I could feel he thought he was doing well as we sped up hill and down dale towards Castleton. I hadn't the heart to let him know there was a tail wind.

I gave him a nasty start when my mudguard came adrift and rubbed on the wheel. That noise had him worried. I shudder when I think of the way he struggled into the wind and rain up those hills on the way back- and so embarrassing as my mates kept passing me!

"Thin on top" managed to retain enough sense this year and actually found the proper way back, although he still had to put lights on to finish. Mind you, he was going round saying what might have been if we hadn't done an extra one kilometre because of road works. I'm worried - I overheard him talking about a 300 km!

Audax - Tour de France style

Raid Pyreneen is a Randonneur route across the backbone of the Pyrenees from the coast of the Atlantic to the Mediterranean. Ivan Waddington, writing in Cycle Chat in 1993, described how he successfully completed this route in June of that year. The distance is 714 kilometres, with 11,000 metres of climbing.

There are 18 cols which include the Col de Tourmalet (a super category climb well known for its inclusion in the Tour de France races) and has a time limit of 100 hours. Ivan's trip proved to be even more difficult, due to the weather conditions he experienced. These ranged from temperatures in the 90s fahrenheit, when a rider had to sit in the shade for some time to cool down enough to continue a climb, to extremely wet and cold. After some long descents, hands had to be prized open from the brake levers

On one occasion Ivan had to stop at a cafe to drink coffee, to regain sufficient control to steer his bicycle for the final 10 kms of the day. It wasn't all like this. He wrote of the fantastic views on some of the climbs - "I cannot adequately convey the sheer excitement and exhilaration of speeding down hill for mile after mile. The only problem is that we dare not take our eyes off the road for more than a second or two for a loss of concentration could be more than a little dangerous."

He recalled the pleasure of cycling in a 'cyclist friendly culture' such as France. In a cafe at the top of one of the cols, the owner would drop whatever he was doing as soon as a cyclist arrived, provide him with liquid refreshment and stamp his brevet card. On leaving, the cyclist was invited, in the best Tour de France fashion, to stuff newspapers up his jersey for the descent. A pile was kept by the proprietor for that purpose.

For the final leg, the group rode together in a carnival atmosphere, maintaining a good pace across fairly flat but uninspiring roads. It made it something like a victory procession. The final 10 miles were ridden in heavy rain, but as Ivan says "By this time, nothing - absolutely nothing - could dampen our spirits."

The man for all meetings

by John Allen

John Allen, the current Leicestershire DA President, has always been a tireless worker on behalf of the CTC. Here he recalls some of the highlights of his cycling career

CTC meetings have always played a major part in my association with this great club of ours. I remember my very first clubrun, which was with the Charnwood section to the Flaxdressers in Ashby de la Zouch for their AGM in October 1954 . My first appearance at a DA committee meeting was not until 1956 when it convened in the Fish and Quart, Churchgate Leicester.

This was a very lively and forthright gathering with the president Bill Seager in the chair. I distinctly remember hiding behind my agenda paper when Bill was in full flow ! Thankfully I was not put off, although I was only 16 at the time, and during the ensuing 40 years I have witnessed many changes and made many friends at section, DA and council meetings.

In 1983, while I was secretary of the DA, all Midland secretaries received a call from the National Secretary, Alan Leng, pointing out that no one had yet been nominated to represent our area on the National Council. To the best of my knowledge, no one from this DA had ever served on council since the consul system ended, J.T. Masser (Nottingham) Jimmy Norman (Nottingham) Fred Williams

(Birmingham) Phil Draper (Willenhall) and Jeanette Woodcock (Surrey) were all previous councillors. New boundaries had been drawn up and Division K comprised of the following DAs: Birmingham and Midland, East Warwickshire, Northamptonshire and Milton Keynes and Leicestershire with one councillor covering the whole area.

At the time of Alan's phone call my duties were DA secretary, Cycle Chat editor, press officer for both the DA and the Charnwood section, also a member of that superb team preparing for the Birthday Rides in August of the following year. I would not have been able to undertake these duties without the support of my wife Ivy, my daughter Julie (then 12) and son Ian (then 8). Our family outfit could be seen on rides most Sundays.

After consultation with my loving family it was decided I should 'go for it' and I sent off for a nomination paper. I took up my duties on the National Council in January 1984 and had a good start. Leicestershire DA had won the Carter Ruck trophy in 1983, this was awarded to the DA judged to be the most successful and as this was the eighties - the most successful decade in our history - I was able, with great pride, to use our own DA as a role model on my visits to other DAs.

Following this I received a national award in February 1984 for my press and publicity work - The Arthur Moss Trophy - (in memory of the late national president) which was presented to me by his widow Elsie. I also received the associated Merit Medallion which was presented to me by Ivy Thorpe the national president at that time. These were presented at the annual council headquarters 'get together' and I accepted them on behalf of our DA without which none of this could have happened.

For my first council meeting the family had bought a new 'posh' briefcase for my papers, but it soon proved to be not nearly large enough. I walked into the committee room at Church House, Westminster not really knowing what to expect. I already knew some members of the council and by 5 pm that Saturday I knew the remainder, as I had been made very welcome by everyone. I was aware beforehand of the many facets covered in the work of the CTC, but to sit on council considering the reports of the different committees and the many council papers on almost anything affecting cycling was mind blowing. There was lively debate and arguments kept in check by a resolute chair-man, Jim Bailey, with everyone having the welfare of the CTC at heart.

The council committees are appointed at the January meeting and I found myself nominated for the DAs and Events committee, on which I was to serve during my eight years on council, four of these years being as chairman. These committees meet separately to council and report back at full council meetings.

From the start, I made it my intention to attend as many DA meetings in the division as possible, this I did and became a member of each one. I missed none of the AGMs, although this meant attending two AGMs on one Sunday, Leicestershire in the morning and Birmingham and Midland in the afternoon! When attending council meetings in London I was able to use the excellent train service from Leicester, but was forced to use my car to get to many of the division meetings when it was just too far to cycle after work (sorry about that!). I saw many changes. The area of Birmingham and Midland was too large, stretching from north of Birmingham to south of Hereford. This has now been made into two DAs, Birmingham and Midland and Hereford and Worcester. Similarly Northants and Milton Keynes is now Northants and North Bucks. Changes were also necessary in some committees.

The 'highs' the 'lows' the successes and the problems, they were all there as they are anywhere else. But the 'highs' for me included the two sponsored rides in aid of the British Lung Foundation. These were joint rides with the CTC, starting from the NEC and going into the Forest of Arden, supported by all the DAs and raising many hundreds of pounds for this worthy cause. All four of the DAs were involved in organising various Birthday Rides during this time and many people I met became and remain very good friends. Their dedication to the CTC was paramount. The 'lows'? Somehow I don't seem able to recall these although, the whingers may have found a small spot in my memories.

I remember with fondness several of those people who made my life richer by their acquaintance and who have sadly died. I still enjoy the company of many others that I can see when out 'up the road.' I stood down after eight years due to pressure of work, but it was with much regret that I did so.

During the eighties the Leicestershire DA was so vibrant that I gave a talk on our activities at the DAs conference held in London during 1984. I fervently hope that we can recapture those philosophies and attitudes for our centenary year and for the start of our next 100 years serving cycling.

The CTC Council in February 1984. Left to right: Bob Carmicheal Riddell, Henry Gregson, Colin Quemby, Ted King, Tim Hughes, Jim Bailey (chairman), Cyril Kermode, Len James, Ivy Thorp, Phil Draper, Derek Roberts, John Allen, Chris Freemantle, Fred Peddle, Paul Stobbs and Keith Matthews.

Bravado ended up with a wet shirt

Why it is that so many tales about cyclists involve water? This story concerns an escapade on a very cold winter's day, when the City section had ridden out to the Atherstone area. It was so cold that the canal had frozen over to a depth that supported the weight of Rob Roulston. However, when a small crack appeared, accompanied with groaning noises he made a hasty jump for the bank.

After laughing at his antics, the group carried on walking along the towpath. At last Rob could stand it no longer and decided that he had chickened out too soon. He got back on to the solid ice once more, but this time the ice broke without warning and deposited Rob into the water. Spare overtrousers and socks were available, but no one had a spare top, so Rob decided to carry on and complete the day out despite being soaking wet above his waist. As far as we know there were no ill effects from this ducking, although he gave canal paths a wide berth for a long while.

* * *

The City section has always had its fair share of characters who go straight into the folklore, one such member is Rob Murray who, it is generally agreed, is no mechanical genius. On one ride he unfortunately got a polythene bag enmeshed in his gears and try as he would he just could not untangle it. With a bit of lateral thinking he concluded that as the chain and gears were metal, it was probably the best idea to burn the bag off. After a wonderful flare up, during which the polythene bag disappeared, he was horrified when he realised that so too had the plastic gear rollers!

Having an (n)ice time on the canal until.....

.....a biker's weight proves too much

Dinners were the roadmen's reward

Campaigning for cyclists has been part of the constitution since the CTC itself was founded in 1878. Although it was to be another 19 years before Leicestershire officially became a DA, much effort was made in this area to uphold the 'rights' of cyclists when prosecutions took place and to preserve their 'rights' to use the highway. These issues were taken up by the chief consul for the county (consuls were volunteers who not only kept an eye open for detrimental reports affecting cyclists, but also kept the national handbook up-dated with regard to catering and accommodation facilities).

One such chief consul was J.Edwin Roper, of Southfields, Leicester, whose initiative led to the formation of the DA. During 1897 Leicester Corporation was seeking powers to arrest cyclists for 'furious riding.' This was opposed by the club.

Mr TJ Webb, the Loughborough consul, was also the first DA president in 1900 and went on to become chief consul and DA chairman, a position he held for the next 18 years. During his first year in office he negotiated for the abolition of dangerous gates across public roads. Much lobbying of local MPs has taken place on behalf of cyclists throughout our history. During 1910, the third DA secretary, JA Hargrave, communicated with all the prospective candidates before the General Election. One of these who successfully retained his seat was Ramsey MacDonald. He had served for a time at the CTC national headquarters as an office boy and went on to become the nation's first ever Labour prime minister.

During our early history the DA organised 'roadmen's dinners' as a mark of appreciation to these maintenance workers who endeavoured to keep the roads in rideable condition. In 1900 one of these dinners was held in Ashby on Friday 2nd February. It was arranged by Mrs E. Pratt and it was chiefly due to her exertions that 50 men, in addition to several road officials, were entertained. Mr D. Hale presided.

On Saturday 18th July 1920, Bernard M'Quillan (DA secretary) organised a North Midland Rally in conjunction with local centres of the NCU and the Notts and Derby DAs at Normanton on Soar. The aim was to show the public that our glorious pastime was very much alive - this was certainly achieved, with 135 participating at the 'Plough' and where Bernard M'Quillan proposed a resolution with an extremely able witty and telling speech. "That this gathering of cyclists emphatically protests against the continued imposition of the purely war-time lighting regulations made under the Defence of the Realm Act. This involving the carrying at night of a red rear light and the lighting of both lamps half an hour after sunset." They wanted to restore the pre-war lighting laws. The motion was carried nem con. and copies of the resolution were sent to every member of Parliament for the counties of Nottingham, Derby and Leicester and also to the Home Secretary and Minister of Transport.

Historical note: The CTC campaigned for many years, and still does, that a person driving any vehicle "should drive at such speed as the way can be seen to be clear." DA secretaries have played a vital role in rights issues, as copies of correspondence and minute books illustrate. Protest meetings against 'present road laws' were held during 1935 across the country, with speed limits and driving at night. These remain even more important today.

Following the Second World War, the committee authorised the DA secretary to take relevant action required and while the M1 motorway was generally approved by cyclists as a means of relieving other roads of traffic we were successful, along with other organisations, in modifying the suggested route to the present one we know today - the original route would have taken even more of the lovely Charnwood Forest.

National Secretary Les Warner was responsible for rights and campaigning in addition to his other duties, a situation which could not be allowed to continue, because of his tremendous work load. Therefore District Associations were asked to appoint rights officers locally and Leicestershire was fortunate in having Ken Pepper, of Barrow on Soar, who had been very interested and involved in rights work for some considerable time. It was largely due to Ken's hard work that cyclists have the right to cross the A46 at Seagrave crossroads as he organised several protest rides in addition to public meetings which gave publicity in the local media.

Ken gave very comprehensive reports at DA meetings, with maps, proposals and other communications from councils. Everyone was aware of potential problems in their own areas. A full-time professional rights officer was appointed nationally during the 1980s, with support staff based at Godalming. This cascaded down into a national rights network of NRN members in all areas of the country co-ordinated by the local rights officers - shades of the old consular system.

Ken stood down in 1992 and proved to be a very hard act to follow. Ron Johnson, of Bagworth, stood in for one year as the co-ordinator until a rights officer could be found. Eric Neal, of Hinckley, who was a very active rights worker in his own area agreed to become our rights officer and has continued to maintain the fine traditions of the DA. It is thanks to him that regular meetings now take place with the road planners and engineers at County Hall, so that cyclists interests are on the agenda for each proposed road building or alteration. Eric's positive, sometimes abrasive, attitude with authorities mirrors much earlier DA campaigners.

Finally "Cycle Campaigning" - terminology which has not dated throughout the last 119 years is to a greater, or lesser, extent to the forefront in member' minds and we are all indebted to our 'champions of the cause.'

Bread and jam to the rescue

We were on our way from the village pub
When we met our local cycling club
And what a magnificent sight
Campanologist David in the lead
All proceeding at moderate speed
Their precision was sheer delight.

Each one attired in appropriate gear
Head well down, elevated the rear
Like a soundless stream they flowed
Two by two in perfect formation
We gazed in utter admiration
At these red arrows of the road.

Round a bend and out of site
Like a flock of geese in silent flight
Disappeared this noble band
And I thought to myself "How excellent"
If everyone on a bicycle went
And no cars allowed in the land.

Just imagine how pure the air would be
No dust and fumes and pollution free
No hedgehogs crushed in vain retreat

Less people hit and maimed, or killed,
For motorists crash however skilled
And policeman back on the beat.

No more gaudy garages spoiling the view
Oil sheiks, oh dear, will lose revenue
And what a reduction in noise
No car workers' stoppages, go slows or strikes
For the long suffering public will all be on bikes
Improving their fitness and poise.

Some thoughts penned by Bernard Laughton, of Lutterworth, on meeting the local section as he returned from bell ringing one Sunday morning in June 1984

He had called for refreshment on his way home for lunch. Thirteen years later these words are as apposite as ever. Doreen Sulley, together with her husband David was the driving force behind the formation of the Lutterworth section in 1982. A group of 19 cyclists had been riding together for about 12 months when they decided to start an official section. Rides were advertised for the first time and the first run was held on 5th December 1982, but with only 11 riders!

Not everyone was happy about changing the informal arrangements and were concerned that the section might grow too large. The rides ,previously led by the Sulleys, were now open to other leaders and there were often long and short rides on the same day. By 17th March 1983 there were 25 riders out on two runs. Eric and Rita Clarke with Peter Milnes gave very valuable help and support seeing the section grow so that on the first birthday 33 riders were on their bikes and 49 on the register.

Robert Sulley researched a ride that had taken place in 1938 when the Lutterworth Cycle Touring Club rode to Chesterton Windmill, in the

Knapton area on Northamptonshire/Warwickshire border. Mr Winnett was a member of this club and has recalled on audio tape some of his memories. These include meetings with Patterson, Wayfarer (WM Robinson) Bill Oakley and Stanley Cotterell, one of the founder members of the CTC.

Cotterell was a bookseller in the Birmingham area and Mr Winnett, a youngster of 17 at that time, frequently rode over to his shop where Stanley told him tales of his early day on his bicycle. Small boys would throw stones and try to throw sticks in to the front wheel of the Ordinaries as the cyclists passed by. Another problem could be local constables, riders travelling at evens, or above, were considered to be 'scorching.' This resulted in an appearance before the magistrates and may even have resulted in a fine. At this time Stanley Cotterell was about 80 years old and full of reminiscences. Ken Winnett became a member of CTC in 1929 and recalls how he lost his wallet. He was

Snow was no deterent to these intrepid Lutterworth section riders, although some preferred to walk

about ten miles from Bangor, intending to make a circular tour around Wales when he discovered that his wallet had been shaken loose from his pocket. He then decided that the only thing he could do was to make his way to the A5 and get back to Lutterworth as soon as possible. Unfortunately the accommodation in Bangor was not a CTC appointment and the breakfast had not been good. He was hungry before he set off, and by the time he reached Cannock he had got 'the bonk'. With no money to buy food, there was not much he could do. He threw his bike down by the roadside and flopped beside it. Two little boys came by and said "Are you alright Mister? He replied that he was just tired. But they must have gone to fetch their mother, because she came down and offered him some bread and jam, that being all she had. Ken Winnett thanked her very much and said he was sorry he couldn't pay her for it. "Don't worry about that" she said. This was just enough to get him home.

His wife reminded him that he could have taken his CTC membership card to the Bangor police who would then have lent him sufficient money to get home. He had managed to make a note of where the boys lived and sent them a gift of money as soon as he got back to Lutterworth. Not everyone in the Lutterworth Touring Club was a member of CTC, some preferred to join the NCU. After hearing these memories, Robert decided to lead the section on a reconstruction of the Chesterton Windmill ride in September 1983.

Lutterworth entered fully into DA events both as participants and as organisers, many of the riders taking some of the awards, from Paul Bicknell (youngest rider) to Peter Milnes (oldest rider). David Sulley was an entrant in final of the BCTC at Chester. Junior BAR was Richard Smith. The Bicknell Family won the Bull Family Trophy. The section won the White Horse picture several times, this is presented to those with most members present at the Chippenham and Cheltenham cycling weekends, held in the Spring. Harry Rigby edited Cycle Chat for many years with Doreen as assistant and distributor. When the carol service came to Countesthorpe, the section provided bell ringers, the choir, solo singers (Joyce Gamble and Harry Rigby) and Heather Fry as one of the readers. Doreen maintains it was really a family section. The Gambles, Smiths, Milnes, Jones, Bicknells, Elphicks as well as the Sulleys, and numerous unattached members swelled the numbers to 67 by 1984.

"We were a healthy, happy crowd, socialising and working together. David was very good at training youngsters in all aspects of DA life. He began to organise treasure hunts to accustom the youngsters to be observant and so give them a head start in events such as the BCTC," said Doreen. She explained how he had devised 'A Star Ride' from Lutterworth which brought the riders back to the start after each 25 mile leg. These became famous, as they were used to encourage people to have a go at the 100 mile events. Many found to their surprise that they had done this distance without really noticing it. Sadly, David died whilst taking part in a DA event, on the 2nd April 1989 at the age of 55. He was much missed by everyone. But his 'star' ride became his memorial when it was run as a sponsored ride in aid of Groby Road Hospital's Link-up campaign for heart patients. This together with collections in churches connected with his bell ringing, and funeral service resulted in over £2000 being handed to the appeal! The section

The Lutterworth section choristers in action

continued under the watchful eyes of Sid and Jenny Smith for a number of years, Sid eventually becoming DA secretary. Harry Rigby moved to Harrogate and the youngsters all went away to college or to work.

CYCLING IS-

-the tingling, and glowing of my cheeks after a crisp Spring ride
-spotting a cluster of snowdrops peeping between the trees
-feeling the warmth of a flask of tea on a cold frosty morning
-finding a bus shelter to rest with my bike when the rain pours down
-the firmness of that hand in the middle of my back, to give me a push up the gruelling slopes,
-the exhilaration of that great descent after the upward climb
-laying in the sun on a grassy canal bank with my bike at my side
-hearing the laughter and chatter of the 'bunch' along a leafy lane
-sipping long cool drinks in the shade of a friendly country pub
-the taste of succulent berries picked from the hedgreow on an Autumn afternoon
-singing carols, pedalling as the first snowflakes fall
-watching the sunset in the distance as we wind our way home
-the relief felt when crossing the Lutterworth sign after a tiring ride
-soaking in a steaming hot bath at the end of the day
- All this, and much more, is cycling....to me.

Heather Fry *(Lutterworth Section February 1983)*

The Birthday Rides are here again

Whose are they? Where are they? and Why are they? Questions which anyone could be forgiven for asking in response to the annual cry "are you going to the Birthday Rides this year?"

It all began in 1970 in response to correspondence in 'Cycletouring' during 1969. It had been suggested by the editor that an event similar to the continental cycle touring meets would be a desirable aim of CTC. Large numbers of cyclists would be seen to be enjoying the act of cycling as opposed to watching others compete. Furthermore it was suggested that the week during which 5th August fell would be most appropriate as it was on that date in 1878 that Stanley Cotterell met with Messrs Ineson and Cunningham in Harrogate to form the Bicycle Touring Club later to be known as the Cyclists' Touring Club.

So, it is the club whose birthday we celebrate - but where? Well, in 1970 the CTC national office in Godalming issued an invitation to come and take part on an informal basis. Families, solo riders, club cyclists or those who had never before ridden with the club all came and rode the week-long event . Some turned up every day, others just for the odd day. It was immediately apparent that this was a popular event and so it was repeated in 1971, again based at Cotterell House, Godalming, this time about 100 took part.

Leicestershire now entered the scene when the venue moved to Loughborough University for 1972. The date (5th August) co-incided with the annual international cycling rally under the auspices of the 'Alliance Internationale de Tourisme' (AIT).

Visitors came from France, Germany, Belgium, Holland, Denmark Sweden and one rider from Japan, who was also able to demonstrate his skills on his unicycle. The Mayor of Loughborough, the cycling Mayor of Grantham, the Sheriff of Nottingham and his lady were all present at opportune times during the week to welcome the club and overseas visitors. One hundred and fifty riders set off from Loughborough's market square on the first day to tour Charnwood Forest.

On the last day, at a dinner at Loughborough University, two young riders, one from Holland and the other from Germany lit 94 candles on a huge cake, leaving the mayors of Grantham, Loughborough and Birkerod (near Copenhagen) to see how long it took them to blow them all out. The President of the AIT's Cycle Touring Commission, Jerzy Przezdziecki, had travelled from Poland for this occasion and gifts, prizes and souvenir plaques were presented and exchanged.

Ken Pepper and Graham Preston were the leading lights of this very successful joint rally and had worked extremely hard to make it the success it undoubtedly proved to be.

The following years venues were: 1973 Bath, 1974 Ipswich, 1975 Shrewsbury, 1976 Alnwick, 1977 Salisbury, 1978 Harrogate (an obvious choice for this the centenary year of the club and also the year in which the AIT came back to Britain, again run as a joint rally) 1979 Ludlow, 1980 Melrose, 1981 Chippenham, 1982 Chester, 1983 Norwich, 1984 Leicester.

It is now obvious that the question 'where' has only one answer - 'anywhere and everywhere.' Leicestershire section members had become accustomed to travelling each year to take part in this wonderful meeting of people from all over the country. People became closer friends as the years passed, and they in turn brought other friends along to enjoy the unique atmosphere.

By 1984 the number of registrations had risen to more than 750 and the organising team found an excellent venue for the event. Scraptoft College was used for accommodation and meals and a neighbouring Rugby club for camping and use of their clubhouse for snack meals. There was also a licensed bar and everyone was so helpful and supportive.

The team was co-ordinated by Morgan Reynolds, with each member taking full responsibility for a certain area. John Williams and John Hough organised the campsite, Ron Johnson drafted out the four daily runs and then arranged the morning coffee stops, lunch venues and afternoon tea stops at appropriate points on each run. This was made easier by the enthusiastic support of numerous WIs in the Leicestershire Federation. Peter Witting and Tony Mellor organised the pre-riding of these routes to produce detailed printed route sheets

This cartoon was specially drawn by Johnny Helms for the 1984 Birthday Rides in Leicestershire

for everyone registered. John Warne took on the responsibility of providing entertainment each night. Most nights provided a choice of two events, a folk group on the first evening, followed on subsequent evenings with a jazz band, lectures on heraldry and archaeology, slide shows, barbecues, a barn dance, brass band and farewell dance together with discos.

On 5th August it is customary to have a formal dinner and this was organised by John and Ivy Allen at Scraptoft College. Also on this day all the rides converged at Illston cricket ground for tea, the largest group of spectators ever recorded for a home game! Unfortunately we have no record of their final score. The birthday cakes required for such a large crowd were all home-made and iced by Fran Hough, with help from her daughter Alison - a total of 13 large rich fruit cakes. This, combined with providing everyone with a cup of tea, was really a mammoth task which the team of DA volunteers handled well.

Extra attractions to the four daily rides were also available, a 'nostalgic' steam rail assisted cycle trip on the Great Central railway between Rothley and Loughborough; a visit to Mercian Cycles at Derby; the TI Raleigh works at Nottingham; Stilton Cheese factory near Melton Mowbray; a ladies shoe factory in Leicester; and Taylors Bell Foundry in Loughborough. These were all booked up very early as there were limits on the numbers that could attend.

On Tuesday 7th August a 200km Audax ride was incorporated into the programme of daily rides, this proved to be popular, with 54 riders entering. The rides each day are designed to suit all ages and capabilities, the A rides being long and fast, the B rides not quite so far and more relaxed, while the C rides are ideal for photographers and cyclists interested in visiting local attractions. The D rides are usually quite short, with young families in mind.

The receiving and recording of all the various combinations of ticket requirements was dealt with by Phyllis Williams and Eileen Johnson. They had to provide tickets for every event and also confirm numbers to caterers, pay accounts and keep a running record for national office of what was being done. Although this is a national event and the bookings go in the first instance to Godalming we found that the DA in fact does all the work. Printers for invitation packs and route sheets had to be found (Leicestershire. County Council helped with the invitation packs and Leicester Community Press with the route cards). Evening events had to be paid for. All this became a nightmare when the national office member of staff responsible for birthday ride bookings, Jill Coppard, was taken ill just as the bulk of members were applying and no information was being sent up to us here.

However, by burning the midnight oil, we were able to retrieve the situation and proceed to putting into envelopes all the tickets required by any one family. Shepshed Post Office played an important part in the success of these Birthday Rides, as the campsite bookings went direct to John Williams, the post master there. The grand envelope stuffing also took place there on their closed afternoon and evening. Seven or eight members of the team arranged themselves around bare tables and began the task of ensuring that Joe Bloggs got his morning coffee, lunch and tea at the correct venues and that he would be admitted to the entertainment of his choice each evening. We also made sure that the tee shirt we provided was in the size that had been ordered!

Yet another task undertaken by the team was to provide large nutritious packed lunches for those not wanting to book ahead. It was felt that as cafes were few and far between in this area, it was a necessary service. In addition, every group leader (there are between 20 - 30 riders in each group) on each ride was given a packed lunch as a thank you. Fresh rolls were delivered to the campsite each morning and a group of willing volunteers began to prepare them at 6.30 am each day. By the end of the week, this wonderful idea seemed not so good after all , but the riders were still delighted with their lunches even if the volunteers were no longer quite so 'willing'.

It is very important to realise that all the work undertaken by the organising committee was not necessarily done by them alone. Each had their own little band of helpers who could be called on for assistance when necessary. An army of leaders was required as the groups of riders like people with local knowledge (and who were familiar with the routes) with them to point out items of interest. We had tremendous support from friends in the wider cycling world, member clubs in the Leicestershire Cyclists' Association all provided help and support during the week along with many more.

Sons, daughters, boy friends, girl friends, wives, husbands. All took holidays from work to lead a run of their choice. We were so grateful for all the support received that it was decided to provide an 'Appreciation Evening' at the Fletcher Building of Leicester Polytechnic. This was paid for with the profits raised by the evening entertainment and 150 people enjoyed a hot buffet meal and entertainment on Saturday 1st December 1984.

As a DA we were extremely proud of everyone who had contributed to providing a hugely successful Birthday Rides, but it was generally agreed that at this level of commitment once was enough. And yet here we are 12 years later staging another series of rides based on Scraptoft College. There is a completely new team of organisers working their way towards what we hope will prove to be an equally successful occasion - even larger than before. In 1996 the number of registrations had risen to 1400 and so the old team look forward to assisting in whatever way they can while leaving room for fresh ideas and enthusiasm of the new team.

John Allen is co-ordinator, Dave Binks is sorting out the four daily rides; Ron Johnson the off road rides and Ray Clay is arranging the campsite with John and Ann Dickinson. Keith and Jean Lakin are sorting out the evening events. Administration is in the hands of Malcolm Keetley; Pat and John Arnold are organising and running the Birthday Tea, with Jean Lakin making and icing the cakes. Arranging the meals on the four daily rides will be a team effort. Lindsey Staples is the researcher for prices on numerous items and has been the motivator from the very beginning.

A chance for the vets to shine

by Morgan Reynolds

The first Triennial Rides held in Leicestershire were on 8th June 1986. These CTC rides are of 100 miles and are restricted to riders aged 50 or over, to be completed within 12 hours. The rides, held every three years, have been in existence nationally for many years. The first was held in 1928. I well remember Jimmy Moulds, a tricyclist from Narborough, who was fiercely proud of his enamel badge with the year tags attached, commemorating his many successes.

In 1986 CTC headquarters at Godalming invited Leicestershire DA to promote the Midland area ride. Birmingham DA, who had always staged it previously, were unable to do so in this year so we took up the challenge - incidentally, the twentieth in the series. So here we were, volunteers Ron Johnson and myself, setting to and planning what was to be a day to remember.

Our event was based on historic Market Bosworth, using the church hall for the duration of the day, with the start point in Bosworth Square. The 85 entrants were arranged into groups of 10 to 12, all with both leaders and sweepers. Starting at 8am in glorious sunny weather on a June Sunday morning, they set off in a south easterly direction through quiet lanes, just touching the border of Northamptonshire before looping back to Bruntingthorpe village hall for welcome elevenses after 34 miles. A further 20 miles brought them back to lunch at Bosworth, by a different route to that of the outward journey.

In the afternoon the route to the north west took in the Trent Valley plus parts of the counties of Derbyshire, Staffordshire and Warwickshire, before arriving at Lullington village hall for tea after 81 miles. The final leg, to complete the figure of eight course, was accomplished between 5.30 and 6.30 pm by all but two of the starters, a wonderful achievement by these veterans of many summers.

Fran Hough co-ordinated a team of willing helpers who had provided refreshments for all DA events throughout the year. They had all excelled themselves on that day and everyone sat down to a super tea at Bosworth.

Milford Blakelock, of Birmingham DA, expressed thanks on behalf of the riders and Ron Johnson, Leicestershire DA President, presented certificates and year bars to all the successful riders. A collection in aid of the British Heart Foundation raised £40, a "thank you" for our ability to enjoy a day to remember.

Three years later, on 14th June 1989, we promoted our second triennial along similar lines to the first, using the same route and venues. We were again blessed with good weather and plenty of helpers. This time Eric Danvers followed the route in his 'back up van' - a real asset in case of mechanical problems.

Rupert and Betty Abbs, popular Loughborough riders, being two of the older riders, ran into some difficulty on the final leg back into Market Bosworth. Betty felt that it was just a bit too far to stoke their tandem. Young Gareth Williams and his cousin, Richard Hough, came to their rescue by riding each side of the tandem, linking arms behind Betty and pedalling. This left the other riders in their group with a struggle to keep up as the four of them disappeared easily off the front. A wonderful achievement for the 'young uns' as well the vets! Chris Davies from Portsmouth D.A. gave a stirring vote of thanks to Leicestershire DA to climax another memorable day.

The rides continued in both 1992 and 1995 in the capable hands of Lyn Stott (nee Bull) who masterminded both events based on Anstey. Figure of eight circuits were still in evidence in 1992 going north-westerly to Coleorton for elevenses, returning to Anstey for lunch, with the afternoon route taking in the Wreake Valley going to Waltham-on-the-Wolds for tea. All these refreshments were organised by the Bull family to the, by now, expected high standard. Les Cross, a national CTC councillor from the north region congratulated the DA and expressed thanks for the whole organisation.

In 1995 there was yet another change of route, going west from the start at the historic Anstey packhorse bridge, taking in the Fenn Lanes on the way to elevenses at Warton. The afternoon circuit journeyed north and east with tea at Wysall before finishing at Anstey Church Hall.

After her sterling work for this DA Lyn has now moved to Derby, leaving space, hopefully, for new faces and ideas for the 1998 Triennial Rides. Long may they continue!

Recipe for War Cake

Published in Cycle Chat in 1992- by Mrs Oulton

Ingredients

One lb plain flour
One oz candied peel
Pinch of salt (can add pepper if liked)
Half lb currants
Half oz cinnamon
One teasp bi-carb
Two tbsps vinegar in half pt of milk.
Half lb sugar.
Half lb hard margarine.

Method

Rub in fat to dry ingredients. Add peel, currants, cinnamon. Add milk and vinegar gradually. Bake for one and threequarter hours at Gas Mark 4 350 F 175 C. No eggs are used due to wartime shortages. But it is interesting to note that the war referred to is The Boer War!.

Source Ray Clay

The 'Cycler' and his tea

This article was taken from Cycling 24th October 1891 and reproduced in Cycle Chat in April 1993

The degeneracy of the necessary repast

The cycler dearly loves his tea. He does not want a sumptuous repast or a palatial hall, neither does he desire a starched and ironed waiter to tower over his chair and make a mental note of his appetite but he does like take ease in some comfortable inn, where he can obtain plain wholesome fayre in good quantities, with the pleasant reflection to aid his digestion that the charge will be moderate as his presence is evidently welcome to the obliging host.

Every little hut nearly that chances to be situated on a popular highway, thinks incumbent on itself to exhibit a notice board bearing the words Cyclers' Rest and on many an inn that once turned up its nose at cyclers, a similar sign is now swinging in the air.

Great, however, as has been the increase in the number of places of refreshment for cyclers, the increase in the number of cyclers to be refreshed has been even greater and when hotel keepers discovered that cyclers were a race of easy going, non fastidious, healthy appetited men, who swarmed down upon them and ate whatever they pleased to give them and paid for a dinner when they had hardly had a tea, they were not too long in taking the hint and many a favourable haunt was spoilt.

It is really a melancholy spectacle to see how the well furnished table at some good old house has gradually become meaner and meaner as the number of customers has increased; while all the old air of comfort and homeliness has disappeared, giving place to a sort of modern shop spirit of make haste, swallow your grub, pay your money and get outside.

This sort of thing that inevitably follows sooner or later when the crowd takes to a place and those who knew it when, from their point of view, it was in its prime, are filled with regret.

News and views in Cycle Chat

The idea for a magazine devoted to the affairs of the DA was first considered in 1929, although it was not until January 1933 that the first issue of Cycle Chat was published. Articles from each section were included as well as details of runs. Among the sections at that time was one for Camping (founded in spring 1931 by Mr R D (Bob) Warner, a lightweight and tandem expert with a shop in Samuel St). Other sections were: Social General, Hinckley and Saturday. Members were informed that a boxing contest was to be held at the clubroom on Friday 3rd Feb and particulars and names were to be with Mr RD Warner by 27th January. Entrance fee 3d. Each section had also provided an article, and a song entitled "Muddy Somewhere" sung to the tune of Widdecombe Fair was published.

The second issue in February reported that the AGM of the DA's Tennis Club was to held at the Secular Hall on 20th February but members were reminded that only Tennis Club members could attend. The ladies page criticised the growing tendency to wear plus fours in the winter and encouraged everyone to stick to shorts the whole year round. Another song "Poor Old Bill" sung to Poor Old Joe told how Bill the cyclist had to hang up his bicycle on finding a wife. A monthly article entitled "Merely by the Way" by 'The Totterer' is reproduced here to give some idea of the flavour:

Now that you have somewhat recovered from the blindness consequent upon the publication of our first number, perhaps you will appreciate the endless store of brains and ideas which you didn't think we had. If only you realised the slavery required to produce such a world shattering journal, you would gladly pay your miserable fourpences out of respect, not even heeding the excellent diet for your withered brains. Even each of the four gentlemen who formed a combine for the purchase of a copy of the magazine would, I trust, give that penny with joyful abandon. One cannot but admire the business talent, but what would happen, should they fail to find sufficient bottles in their favourite dustbin?

We would be glad of your criticisms regarding the magazine; by criticisms we mean criticisms, as of course, we wish to do our best for all our readers. Pardon me!, the Editor's halo has dropped rakishly over one ear. It has been said, amongst other things, that more space should be allotted to cycling matters. Well, I can soon oblige. How about a little homily on cycling for beginners? Here goes !

The joy of cycling is best achieved by the possession of a cycle. This should consist of two wheels set at intervals along a framework of what is called chrome-molybdenum steel. Gaspipes will do, but the maker knows best. I have always found it advisable to have all joints brazed, they hold together better. On the hind end of this framework is mounted a terrible affair known as a saddle, which is useful for catching the sufferer on his downward journey. The other end is bedecked with more piping termed handlebars, varying from three inches to three feet in width. These are gripped frantically by both hands. The lower half of the doings is provided with pedals, which when each tenanted by a foot, and shoved and pushed alternately up and down, provide a powerful rotary motion to the rear wheel. I should have mentioned that the wheels are generally circular, and garnished with pieces of scrap rubber known as tyres. The owner, now having graduated from the theoretical course, may mount by placing the left foot in the left pedal, throwing the right leg over to the other side of the contraption, and crashing gently into the saddle. During this delicate operation the handlebars are generally held. On no account bring the left leg up to the right while in the act of mounting, and remember, left leg, left pedal, or the rider will not only find himself in a false position, but also in the police station, furtively eyeing the chalk-line. Having correctly gained the saddle, attempts should be made to impart the aforementioned motion to the rearwheel. The whole affair will then proceed in a forward direction, with the rider spread out all over it, and clinging desperately to the handlebars. To turn to the right, jerk the right hand end of the piping, and to turn left tug at the opposite end. Providing the bars remain contiguous with the frame, the objective will be gained; should they not, then something will happen and you'll be it. The joy mentioned will be apparent up to about ten miles, after which you will return home and gaze at the advertisements which have stung you, and wonder why. Then some-true friend will come along and introduce you to the General Section's Tours, after which you will not need your cycle, a time table for George Stephenson's tandem will suffice.

The issue for March 1933 contained heated debate on whether girls should serve on committee (not only opposed by the men) although one ex committee man wrote to complain that when he had been on committee some years before, the only contribution two ladies made was the "click click click of their knitting pins." Nature notes and photographic notes appeared and 'The Totterer' took issue with the shorts debate. He maintained "one can go anywhere in plus fours but I defy anyone wearing shorts to enter a hotel which has a good class clientele." He concluded with a rhyme for the children

Mary has a little lamb
Her father shot it dead
But still it goes with her to school
Between two bits of bread.

April's issue continued the cycling and camera notes and recorded that the Camping section was also using youth hostels. There were no songs or rhymes but Lilian F Jesson (cousin to Florrie Wilson) took issue with 'The Totterer' claiming to have entered the best hotels wearing shorts, accompanied by her husband, without any problems at all.

In June Leicestershire Road Club reported on the racing season and members were begged to attend an Inter DA Gymkhana to be held at Wymeswold on 1st July. Thursday evening runs were started as an experiment and the 'girls on committee' correspondence still rumbled on.

In July a blow fell. The editorial read: "We regret to inform you that the bottom has dropped out of Cycle Chat." This proved to be the final issue for a while. In it the club librarian Mr C Record (!) offered the hire of maps for holiday tours at 3d per map per week.

The magazine appeared very spasmodically over the following years until 1981 when it was re-issued in its present form as a quarterly record of happenings in the DA with Peter Hopkins and John Allen as joint editors. Cycle Chat has since enjoyed an unbroken run of four issues each year. Editors have been John Allen (Jan 83 - Oct 84) Harry Rigby (Jan 85 - Oct 94) The committee was warned in January 1994

The cover of the very first edition of Cycle Chat which was published in January 1933

that this was the last year Harry could edit Cycle Chat as he was moving to Harrogate. No one offered to take on the job, so Harry produced an emergency edition for January 1995, in between emptying his house and transporting everything to Harrogate.

The way the magazine is produced means that access to a computer is a great help, so those who work with computers, or who own one, feel under pressure to help out. Peter Witting very nobly stepped into the breach for the April to October issues despite being under a lot of pressure at work due to changes in the location for his job.

In January 1996, Ken Hoxley who had retired from his work as a journalist and who had produced the British Gas in house magazine for some time agreed to become joint editor with Peter. He finally took over the full editorship and is attracting new contributors in each issue.

The printing of Cycle Chat is now in the capable hands of a volunteer group belonging to the Trinity Methodist Church Loughborough. They work from a well equipped print room producing work for non profit making organisations. Ray Clay, the current secretary, introduced us to them when Harry left for Harrogate.

Harry had produced Cycle Chat on a computer at the school where he had taught for some years. Early editions were produced for John Allen through the good offices of someone in the Nottinghamshire area. This of course meant that John had some distance to travel to take the copy and collect the magazines.

Distribution and administration, including the accounts, has been the responsibility of Eileen Johnson since January 1992. She took over from Lyn Bull who had done this job from January 1991. She had, in turn, taken over from Doreen Sulley of Lutterworth. Doreen also acted as assistant editor to Harry, taking over from Iain Bell of Coalville in January 1986 who had held this position for a year. Previously the job had been done by John Williams of Shepshed who had assisted John Allen and Peter Hopkins from the renaissance of the magazine in 1981.

The other man's grass....

Cyclists have always been keen to visit different locations and many like to explore countries with customs, language and scenery which cannot be found in the UK. Very early in our history the committee was required to agree with the railway company rates for cyclists, to take themselves and their cycles to districts which couldn't be reached by bike in the time they had available from work.

This arrangement extended to some of the ferry companies as well, members being able to specify 'CTC rates' when booking their tickets. So, in the 1900s, began the habit of taking off to pastures new. Often arrangements were made to meet other cyclists at the destination and enjoy a day exploring their lanes and byways, having lunch and tea with them and making new friends. This was still a common practice after the Second World War and on into the 1950s and 60s.

During the 1950s Ron and Eileen Johnson, regularly caught the evening train from London Road station to north Derbyshire. This meant taking cycling clothes to work as there was only just enough time to get to the station before the train left. Once on the train, the first dinner sitting was usually called after the stop at Loughborough. Provided you explained to the waiter, he would rush the meal along so that it was finished by the time the train arrived at Chinley. Here there was a choice of either cycling to your destination or catching the local train into Edale. If they were visiting southern Derbyshire the Friday procedure was exactly the same, but instead of catching the train they cycled up to Shining Cliff or Overton Hall Youth Hostel to get a good start for Saturday. Sunday was always spent riding back to Leicester.

This pattern was repeated for Bank Holiday weekends and the annual fortnight from work. It was usual up until the 60s for everyone to have to take their annual break at the same time. The first two weeks in August in the case of Leicester. Eric Neal, of Hinckley, Ron Johnson and Eileen Wilson joined forces in the mid 50s to tour north and western Scotland. Because everyone had the same holiday period the transport system was under great strain. The stations were a seething mass of people waiting to go to the destination of their choice.

Immediately after the war it was even worse, as everyone wanted to get away from it all and were keen to visit the seaside towns which had been closed to them for so long. Consequently long queues formed at the three Leicester stations, London Road, Great Central Street and Belgrave Road (for the East coast). The queues would stretch out of the station and along the street, and it was often impossible to find a seat on the train. Corridor journeys were very common then.

However, things were much improved by the time Ron, Eileen and Eric met on the platform for a journey to Northern Scotland. This was an annual trip for Ron and Eileen as they had often taken the sleeper to Glasgow and either cycled from there or taken another train further north. This time the journey was to last from Friday evening until late on Saturday afternoon, as various trains took them up to Bonar Bridge. It was on this holiday that they met Bill Bones, secretary of the Rough Stuff Fellowship.

Scotland was a favourite venue for many DA riders over the years as many photographs and slide shows testify. There must be many reading this book who remember the midges. Eileen once asked an elderly Scottish lady, dressed in the local fashion of black from head to toe what remedy the locals recommended to stop them. She turned, looked at Eileen's short shorts and sleeveless arms, and said dismissively, in a very broad accent "We cover ourselves up lassie."

Eric Neal and Eileen Wilson avoid the midges during a lunch time brew up on the Primus

Eric has written elsewhere of his experiences as a tour leader. He has also joined many other CTC tours, visiting many countries in the process. These tours are not, in fact, organised by the CTC but by the people leading them. A lot of hard work goes into researching foreign countries and booking accommodation on behalf of the ordinary members, all of whom are entitled to go.

Ron and Eileen have taken advantage of this with a holiday to Nepal in 1989 and one to China in 1992. Out of these tours has grown a nationwide group of cyclists who regularly meet to take holidays, offer hospitality in their own areas, meet at the York and Mildenhall Rallys each year and generally enjoy each other's company.

In 1990 Ron and Eileen were asked if they would like to be part of a group of eight cyclists invited to Russia. A Russian government department paid for all the accommodation, food and travel within Russia. They also paid the entrance fees for visits to the State Circus and museums etc. Russian cyclists were allowed to take the British cyclists into their homes as guests. This was the beginning of

Perestroika. The party cycled, camped, hostelled and stayed in hotels on their journey around the Golden Ring cities. The only restriction placed on them during the whole two weeks was not to take photographs as they cycled through the centre of what was obviously a combined army and airforce base. Photographing trains was also strictly forbidden, even nearly derelict steam engines in a siding, as one of the party discovered as he was marched off to explain himself.

Because of the wonderful hospitality and friendship encountered in Russia, it was decided to invite the Russian cyclists to England. Eileen explained: "Needless to say there was no friendly government department we could appeal to for help and so the eight of us decided to go ahead alone". The first obstacle was the visa. To obtain an exit visa the Russians needed a British entry visa. Unless they could show that they could afford to come and support themselves while here, and would leave at the end of the three weeks, there was no chance of obtaining them. Each of the eight UK cyclists then had to formally invite one of the Russians and to accept full responsibility for that person while he or she was in England. This had to be legally sworn at a solicitor registered as a Notary Public. A Loughborough solicitor kindly nipped back out of retirement to help out Ron & Eileen.

Having crossed this hurdle everything went well, with the eight Russians finally arriving for a two week tour. They stayed in hostels at Jordans and Stratford, then went via Bath to the south coast at Beer and back into the Thames Valley to spend the last few days commuting into London from Walton on Thames. There they all camped at the home of Clive Williamson, one of the original eight British cyclists.

During the ride around England there were some anxious moments when the groups became separated. Their English was not too good and they could not get used to the fact that there were so many side roads. They tended to just keep going along any road they happened to be on. One lunchtime Ron had to persuade a local garage to get their car out and drive around the lanes at Bidford on Avon until one little group was located. Vlad,who had very little English, became separated as we approached Street. He stopped to ask a passing lady the way to the hostel. She was able to give him comprehensive instructions in Russian!

Charnwood section pioneered another way of really getting to know cyclists from other countries when they became members of Coalville Town Twinning Association. They had received an invitation from their twin town Romans sur Isere for cyclists to join a Spring Tour which takes place each year at Pentecost. Ron Johnson was the only one able to go at that time and so set off in the bus from Coalville, together with other English visitors. Fortunately for those of us who were not able to go, this proved to be a very tough tour indeed. Ron was collected as soon as the bus arrived in Romans and was not seen again until it was time for the bus to return to Coalville. During this time he hung on as best he could to a bunch of very fit racing cyclists as they whisked him up and down six cols on the first day, followed on the second day by the Ventoux (of Tommy Simpson fame) the Col des Aires and the Col de Macuegne. The third and final day consisted of more or less a race back, taking in any bumps which were on their route. Ron's shorts and chamois lining were worn into strips, looking just like a vertical blind, by the end of this tour.

It was obvious that this type of cycling was not suited to most Charnwood members and so arrangements were made to twin with the touring club of Romans, Velo Touristique Romanais Peageois (VTRP). Romans sur Isere is ideally situated, being in the valley of the river with the mountains of the Vercors about 10-15 miles away. This provides terrain for everyone to enjoy their cycling and is a beautiful part of France.

The first year, 1985, ten Charnwood members joined the Town Twinning trip for the early May Bank Holiday trip, staying in the homes of their French hosts. In subsequent years Alain Villard, an employee of a local French government department, made arrangements for us to hire a hostel on the banks of the river Isere, at the 'Base Nautique,' which is a national centre of excellence for rowing. Meals were arranged at an old people's home in the town. This did not fill them with confidence until they arrived and sampled the meals. In fact, most decided to book beds for their declining years there and then! Numbers going to France increased each year and transport moved on from a mini bus and trailer to a coach. They even persuaded the coach driver to try cycling while he was there and made an instant convert. He had a wonderful holiday while being paid to be there - the ultimate achievement.

During this time some of the English were invited to join with the VTRP cyclists on a visit to one of their other twin towns, Zadar in Yugoslavia. Ron and Eileen, Mike Gould, Trevor Staples and Dave Roche jumped at this opportunity to visit a country very close to descriptions found in fairy tales. One experience, a bit too close, was when Sandrine, the youngest daughter of Alain and Lydia Villard, became lost in the market square. Lydia was quite distraught as there were many gypsies about and she feared that her small, fair haired daughter had been lured away. Luckily she had merely seen another French family she knew and had skipped away to join them.

Plitvice national park, an area of water. streams, waterfalls and karst pools reinforced the image of fairyland, and a group of gypsies by the wayside, complete with dancing bears, made the riders wonder if they had really slipped into the pages of a storybook.

The link with VTRP is still strong, with small groups going from Loughborough section. There has been no DA trip for some years as no one has volunteered to organise it, but the opportunity is still there.

Yet another form of travel has been developed by an enterprising bus company from Tyneside. With Bike Express a luxury coach tows a purpose built trailer for bicycles and tandems and travels down the Al, M18, Ml then on down to the Channel ports. Tickets are booked from the nearest convenient motorway service area to a similar service area en route in France. Spain and Italy are also on their itinerary, thus providing an excellent choice of destinations.To celebrate our centenary, Morgan Reynolds is organising a trip in early May to Orgon in Provence. Thirteen DA members are booked on the two week trip.

When Ron and Eileen retired in January 1995, they had the idea of celebrating their freedom by travelling farther afield. New Zealand was the country chosen and they offered to make all the bookings for anyone wanting to go. The final group was Ron and Eileen, Morgan and Joy Reynolds, Eric Danvers, Keith and Diana Wileman (Portsmouth DA) and John and Jenny Hockley (members from Cheltenham).

"Four weeks cycling around South Island, followed by three weeks touring North Island (in a hired mini bus as they were running out of time) proved to be an excellent introduction to this novel idea of not having to go to work each day," said Eileen.

"Our experiences there would fill a book (as they say) but one I particularly recall is of crossing the Christchurch Plain after two days of such headwinds that we could barely make five miles an hour. Indeed we had to walk down into the Raikia Gorge as we were blown off our feet.

Then we turned (at Windwhistle Corner) and the wind was behind us - bliss". This continued the next day when Morgan and Eric noticed that at 20 miles they were doing 20mph. And so a challenge was born. At 21 miles, 21mph: 22 miles, 22mph and so across flat countryside with no downhill gradients to help until they failed at 25 miles because they were already riding at 27mph. They got back on course through 26, 27, 28 and 29 miles, but the game was brought to a halt at 30miles as they entered a small town and found a lunch stop.

Dick Thompson, of Charnwood, is a keen traveller, visiting Eastern Europe, North Africa, and South America during his CTC trips, sometimes in the company of Eric Neal. Anne and John Dickinson, also of Charnwood section, have cycled in Iceland in addition to numerous other countries. Loughborough section members enjoy taking their bicycles to Spain, Portugal and Eastern Europe as well as the nearer EEC countries.

Ken Pepper is a staunch supporter of the AIT (Alliance Internationale de Tourisme) Rally which is hosted each year by a different country.

Ken organised the 1972 rally held in Loughborough and has taken many DA members with him over the years on his visits to Holland, Germany, Poland, Czechoslovakia, Hungary and Japan among others.

Majorca is the mecca each year in early spring for cyclists from all over Europe and the British Isles, travelling to get some early training rides in the warm sunshine. Touring cyclists have found that it is a beautiful island full of wild flowers and mountain scenery, with little used roads and historic towns. Once, that is, you have escaped from the coastal strip on which package tour operators put their hotels. One of the worst coastal towns must be Arenal, and yet only three streets back from the coast road you are into the beautiful countryside. Palma is within easy cycling distance, as is the Soller Pass, the route to the other side of the island. The advantage of a base at Arenal is that the package cost is often cheaper than staying elsewhere on the island. Puerto Pollensa is at the top of the island in the most beautiful mountain scenery. Barbara and Peter Witting, Ken and Wendy Hoxley, Morgan and Joy Reynolds, Ron and Eileen Johnson, Dave Binks and Janet Preston have all ridden in this lovely island.

Holland is one of the easiest countries in which to ride a bicycle. There are cyclists' roads, traffic lights, bridges across canals and rivers, signposts and places to park your bike to explore the quaint towns and villages on foot. Everyone is cyclist friendly, although the same cannot be said for the language. Menus are not easy, Eileen almost decided to give up when she discovered that cream translates into slagroom! But the food is good particularly in hostels. When attending the Tandem Club international rally some time ago Diana (Portsmouth DA) and Eileen plucked up sufficient courage to join a queue in the market place, eventually they were able to buy a bread roll containing raw herring. One between them seemed enough at the time, but it proved to be surprisingly tasty, it was a pity the queue was so long.

Many people and countries and stories have been left out of this account. Some of them due to space, but a lot of them because no one wrote or told us about them. Bill Seager tells of his foreign tours, with friends, from the late 40s on. We know by hearsay of others. How did Bernard

Brittain get home when he came off his bike and broke his collar bone on the first day of a tour in an Eastern European country? What were Eric Neal's impressions of Japan? He must have liked it as he has been for a second visit. What really happened in South America when the CTC tour leader didn't take cash with him, only to find that his credit cards were not acceptable there? Dick Thompson knows!

What a wonderful life we are privileged to lead as cyclists.... someone really ought to write a book!

Filling water bottles at the well at Sintra, Portugal in 1994

Appendix

DA Officials over 100 years

	Secretary	President
1897	George L Berry	-
1898	George L Berry	-
1899	George L Berry	-
1900	George L Berry	-
1901	George L Berry	TJ Webb
1902	George L Berry	TJ Webb
1903	George L Berry	TJ Webb
1904	George L Berry	TJ Webb
1905	George L Berry	TJ Webb
1906	George L Berry	TJ Webb
1907	AW Wilkinson	TJ Webb
1908	JA Hargrave	TJ Webb
1909	JA Hargrave	TJ Webb
1910	BL M'Quillin	TJ Webb
1911	BL M'Quillin	TJ Webb
1912	BL M'Quillin	TJ Webb
1913	BL McQuillan	TJ Webb
1914	BL M'Quillin	TJ Webb
1915	BL M'Quillin	TJ Webb
1916	BL M'Quillin	TJ Webb
1917	BL M'Quillin	TJ Webb
1918	BL M'Quillin	TJ Webb
1919	BL M'Quillin	CH Garner
1920	BL M'Quillin	CH Garner
1921	BL M'Quillin	FCW Stevenson
1922	BL M'Quillin	FCW Stevenson
1923	BL M'Quillin	-
1924	Chas H Garner	-
1925	Chas H Garner	BL M'Quillin

	Secretary	President
1926	Chas H Garner	BL M'Quillin
1927	Chas H Garner	BL M'Quillin
1928	RE Timson	BL M'Quillin
1929	RE Timson	BL M'Quillin
1930	NF Coleman	BL M'Quillin
1931	NF Coleman	CR Robson
1932	SJ Gibson	CR Robson
1933	SJ Gibson	CR Robson
1934	C Fisher	S Leeson
1935	SJ Gibson	S Leeson
1936	SJ Gibson	S Leeson
1937	SJ Gibson	S Leeson
1938	FE Whitmore	TP Gannon
1939	FE Whitmore	TP Gannon
1940	FE Whitmore	TP Gannon
1941	GE Markham	TP Gannon
1942	GE Markham	SPV Bray
1943	GE Markham	SPV Bray
1944	GE Markham	B Warner
1945	GE Markham	B Warner
1946	GE Markham	B Warner
1947	GE Markham	B Warner
1948	GE Markham	J Jackson
1949	H Oldham	J Jackson
1950	FV Forryan	J Jackson
1951	FV Forryan	J Jackson
1952	K Pepper	A White
1953	K Pepper	A White
1954	EM Clark	A White

	Secretary	President
1955	EM Clark	A White
1956	EM Clark	TW Seager
1957	EM Clark	TW Seager
1958	ED Broom	TW Seager
1959	ED Broom	TW Seager
1960	ED Broom	TW Seager
1961	ED Broom	EM Clark
1962	ED Broom	SA Mottram
1963	RW Thorp	SA Mottram
1964	RW Thorp	SA Mottram
1965	RW Thorp	SA Mottram
1966	RW Thorp	SA Mottram
1967	RW Thorp	SA Mottram
1968	RW Thorp	SA Mottram
1969	BN Broom	SA Mottram
1970	BN Broom	SA Mottram
1971	BN Broom	RW Thorp
1972	D Heggs	RW Thorp
1973	D Heggs	RW Thorp
1974	D Heggs	RW Thorp
1975	J& A Hartshorne	SA Mottram
1976	J& A Hartshorne	SA Mottram
1977	E Neal	PA Allen
1978	E Neal	PA Allen
1979	E Neal	H Naylor
1980	E Neal	H Naylor
1981	JF Allen	E Neal
1982	JF Allen	E Neal
1983	JF Allen	K Pepper
1984	JF Allen	K Pepper
1985	JF Allen	R Johnson
1986	Mrs E Johnson	R Johnson
1987	Mrs E Johnson	M Reynolds
1988	Mrs E Johnson	M Reynolds
1989	S Smith	P Witting
1990	S Smith	P Witting
1991	S Smith	D Heggs
1992	Ms L Stott	D Heggs
1993	Ms L Stott	Mrs E Johnson
1994	Ms L Stott	Mrs E Johnson
1995	Ms L Stott	JF Allen
1996	R Clay	JF Allen
1997	R Clay	JF Allen

National Events organised by the DA

British Cycle Touring Competition: The DA organised a heat every year from its inception in 1952 until the end of the competition in May 1994

BCTC National Finals: 1953, 1963, 1975, 1987

National Dinner: 1976 and 1987

AIT Rally: 1972

Birthday Rides: 1972, 1984, 1997

Vets' Triennial rides: 1986, 1989, 1992, 1995

National Awards gained by the DA and its members

Carter Ruck Trophy (most successful DA): 1964, 1979, 1983, 1985

YORK RALLY
Family outfit Trophy: 1970/71 The Reynolds family
1981 The Allen family

Sir Alfred Bird Memorial Prize
1986 Ken Pepper

Arthur Moss Memorial Trophy and Merit Medallion (Successor to the Sir Alfred Bird Trophy)
1983 John Allen

Certificates of Merit
1976 Phil Allen
1983 Tom Seager
1986 John Allen
1986 John Allen (August)
1986 L Brigstock (November)
1987 Eric Neal (National Dinner)
1097 Morgan Reynolds (National Dinner)
1992 Ron and Eileen Johnson (December)

BCTC FINAL:

Winner (Brooks Trophy)

1970 David Gelder
1987 John Allen
1994 Peter Witting

First novice (Redditch Trophy)

1975 Martyn Cowlyn
1976 Peter Witting
1986 Harry Rigby
1987 Kim Suffolk

First woman

1989 Lynn Bull
1994 Lynn Bull

First junior

1994 Katie Keetley

DISTRICT ASSOCIATIONS' TOURIST COMPETTION

Men's winner

1993 Kim Suffolk
1995 Kim Suffolk
1996 Kim Suffolk

Women's winner

1994 Lynn Bull

First junior boy

1992 Ben Keetley
1993 Ben Keetley

First junior girl

1994 Katie Keetley
1995 Katie Keetley
1996 Katie Keetley

Acknowledgments

The editor, Ken Hoxley, and compilers, Eileen Johnson and Janet Jones, gratefully acknowledge contributions from the following people:

John Allen, Phil Allen, Vince Bicknell, Mollie Blower, Rhona and Bernard Brittain, Frank Coulson, Frank Forryan, Heather Fry, Janet and Sam Gabbitas, Joyce Hames, Alan Hartshorne, Adele Heafield, Dennis Heggs, Nancy Holden, Peter Hopkins, Ron Johnson, Keith Lakin, Bernard Laughton, Phil Liggett, Mary Margoschis, William Moore, Jeff Morant, Howard Naylor, Eric Neal, Kath Nickels, Stephen Ralphs, Brenda Randon, Morgan Reynolds, Nick Rosenthal, Bill and Connie Seager, Doreen Sulley, Alan Tyrell, Ivan Waddington, John and Phyllis Williams, Florrie Wilson, Peter Witting and Anita Wykes.

Invaluable help in various ways was also given by:
Keith Wileman - Portsmouth DA archivist (use of early Gazettes); 90th Anniversary souvenir book compiler - John Allen, Keith, Jean and Leila Lakin for the use of their word processor; Ken and Wendy Hoxley for use of computer equipment (and home). TeamPrint - production

The producers express sincere thanks to the following who pre-subscribed to this book:

Ian Allen
John and Ivy Allen
Phil and Anne Allen
Richard Barber
Claire James and Tom Bell
Owen and Mollie Blower
David Bousfield
Rhona and Bernard Brittain
Betty Broom
Martin Bulmer
J R Catt
Ray and Penny Clay
Pam Cottle
Richard Daniells
Anne, Eric and Fraser Danvers
Roy and Ian Dayman
Roy Deacon
John and Ann Dickinson
Philip Ennis
Wally Farnham
Heather and Nigel Fry
Frank Forryan
Sam and Janet Gabbitas
Michael and Alan Gayler
Kevin Groocock
Joyce and Arthur Hames
Alan Hartshorne
John and Anne Hartshorne
Adele D Heafield
Dennis Heggs
Steve Hill
Nancy Holden
Peter and Margaret Hopkins
D Hurst
Ron and Eileen Johnson
Arthur and Anthony Jones
Stan and Nancy Kent
David King
Leicestershire Record Office
Keith, Jean and Leila Lakin
Olwen Livingston
Wilf Martin
William K Moore
Jeff Morant
Howard and Betty Naylor
Eric and Janet Neal
Loic Pierre (France)
Ethel E Pickering
Brenda Randon
Joy and Morgan Reynolds
Bill and Connie Seager
Ken Sharpe
Ann Sparham (Australia)
Sid and Cathy Standard
Trevor, Lindsey and Timothy Staples
Doreen Sulley
Robert and Fiona Sulley
Alex Thomson
Andrew Tokeley
A Trowell
Julie Tsang
Alan W Tyrell
Ivan Waddington
S C Warrington
S A Wheldon
E J Whitehead
John, Phyl and Gareth Williams
Florrie Wilson
Peter and Barbara Witting
Anita and Terry Wykes